JOURNEY
TO THE CROSS
A REFLECTIVE LENTEN DEVOTIONAL

JON JENNINGS

First paperback edition December 2023

Cover design and formatting by Julie V. Miser
Author Photograph by Patricia Santangelo

ISBN 979-8-9888818-2-7 (paperback)
ISBN 979-8-9888818-3-4 (ebook)

jonjennings.me

For Chris, Cayla, Chad, Chandler, and Charity

My Fab-5:

Because you have shown me the heart of the Father

for His children

FOREWORD

IT WAS THE LAST BAPTISM OF THE YEAR, and around New Hope Church, baptism is one big party! We celebrate greatly as we love watching people say yes to Jesus and go public with their faith. As I watched 35 people being baptized by our team, I looked over and saw my great friend of 25 years, Pastor Jon Jennings, with tears pouring down his face as he celebrated each individual coming out of the water and beaming with a victorious smile. He was my guest speaker that weekend and he had worked exhaustively, yet he proceeded to lend his heart and his tears to the lives of people he didn't even know.

It affected me because this is not the same Jon I've known over the years. There's a different air to this man that only something transformative could have accomplished. He is new and it is contagious. He speaks boldly with passion and compassion. He writes with a deep conviction, and he listens with great intention because he cares.

The Journey Series Jon is writing comes from this place of transformation, and I am so glad he is sharing his revelation with us through this series of books so that we might encounter a similar life change. I loved *Journey to the Manger* and the people in our church couldn't wait to have it themselves. We sold several hundred copies during the Advent season and are expectant to see a pivotal shift among them.

I am beyond excited that Jon has followed up with his book Journey to the Cross. It offers a completion to the story that highlights the reason for it all, Jesus' sacrifice for our salvation. Jon has gifted us with yet another gem packed full of inspiration as we follow Jesus' journey to the cross during the season of Lent. We tend to casually pass by the most important seasons of our Christian faith, and I love that Jon invites us to experience the journey Jesus took, so we might follow him and learn. As a pastor and a friend, I am taking full advantage of Jon's brilliant insights and putting them into my congregation's hands. No one should miss out on this book because he has taken difficult topics to comprehend and made them easy to grasp.

To be honest, the only challenge with this book is that I had to limit myself to a devotion a day. I couldn't put it down. I strongly encourage you to read Jon's work, but when you do, take your time, and reflect. Practice silence, invite Jesus to be with you, pray, and then journal your thoughts. Do this and watch your life transform before your eyes. If you apply the practices that Jon has outlined but also dive into the message of each day's devotion, you will find yourself on a pathway to Freedom that leads to Jesus.

I will never forget seeing Jon as he wept with gratitude for the people who were baptized and saved. I will never forget the sight of the cross in our auditorium guarding the baptismal, a promise of restoration. The moment I saw these things, an old hymn filled my heart - "So I'll cherish the old rugged cross…I will cling to the old rugged cross." Jon, thank you for reminding us of that Cross and how to cling to it as we pursue the freedom that Jesus paid for.

Joe Skiles Jr.
Senior Pastor
New Hope Church – Concord, CA

AUTHOR'S PREFACE AND HOW TO USE THIS DEVOTIONAL

A COMMON PRACTICE in our modern era is a 21-day season of prayer and fasting to begin the new year. Many churches and believers have found life through this intentional time in January for spiritual renewal and missional focus, but dedicated times of prayer and fasting are not new to Christianity. One such practice is the 46-day period leading up to Easter known as Lent.

Lent, from the Old English word *"lencten"* simply means "springtime" or "spring." "Lencten" hails from an earlier Germanic word *"langitinaz"* meaning "lengthening of the day" to reflect the transition from the deadness of winter to the newness of life found in spring. From as early as the 4th century, Lent has been utilized by Christians for a time of covenant renewal where hearts are sanctified, and minds are prepared to behold the risen Christ at Easter. Notes from the Council of Nicaea in 325 CE reveal a 40-day fast was common for catechumens preparing for Easter baptisms and although the traditions varied from region to region, by the 6th century these traditions had merged into a single practice. There is evidence from the writings of Irenaeus, Bishop of Lyons, in the 2nd century indicating this 40-day pre-Easter fast reached as far back as the Apostolic era, thereby, making it one of the oldest practices in Christianity.

The focus of the Lenten season is personal holiness as one

walks with Christ to the cross. The bar of discipleship is raised high on this journey as Jesus challenges His followers to take up their own cross and learn more deeply what it means to follow the crucified Lord. Jesus' fasting for 40 days in the wilderness to prepare Him for ministry is the model which is followed in this season. Through the journey to the cross, we are invited to repent before Him, suffer with Him, abide in Him, and experience resurrection life through Him.

We begin the journey to the cross with an invitation to know Christ and become one with Him. We then move to Caesarea Philippi where Peter confessed Christ as Lord, and Jesus spoke plainly of His death. We walk with the Savior as He sets His face toward Jerusalem, teaches His disciples, performs miracles, and confronts religious leaders. We end in Jerusalem to experience the passion of Christ and His triumph over sin and death. For followers of Jesus, this is a time of preparation for what is to come and to experience the full glory of the finished work of Christ.

I encourage you to practice the spiritual disciple of fasting as you walk this journey. Fasting is abstaining from something physical to gain something spiritual and allows us to seek the Lord for breakthrough in our own lives as well as the world around us. The words of the Lord through the prophet Isaiah paint a beautiful picture of what fasting can do.

"Is not this the kind of fasting I have chosen: to loose the chains of injustice and untie the cords of the yoke, to set the oppressed free and break every yoke? Is it not to share your food with the hungry and to provide the poor wanderer with shelter—when you see the naked, to clothe them, and not to turn away from your own flesh and blood? Then your light will break forth like the dawn, and your healing will quickly appear; then your righteousness will go before you, and the glory of the LORD will be your rear guard. Then you will call, and the LORD will answer; you will cry for help, and he will say: Here am I."

(Isaiah 58:6-9 NIV)

Ask the Lord in this season what kind of fast He is choosing for your life. It may be fasting one day per week, one meal per day for the 40 days, or abstaining from something for the entire Lenten season. I encourage you to follow God's prompting and be obedient to His voice.

Journey to the Cross was written from my daily journal and follows the traditional Lenten calendar of the church. Growing up Pentecostal, I knew little of the historical calendar or the practices Christians have observed for centuries, but once I discovered them, I realized these are not empty rituals, but rather, full of life and spiritual depth. As you engage with this content, I invite you to take a bold step and change how you engage with God daily. See yourself entering a sacred mystery where awe and wonder dominate your time. This devotional is designed for deep reflection, not a quick fix so you can check the box as you rush out the door each morning. I recommend the following practice to get the most out of the devotional content.

1. **Slow Down.** Put your devices in another room and find a serene, quiet place.

2. **Practice Silence.** This will be uncomfortable at first if you have never done it, but it helps clear out the noise and clutter that compete for our attention. Try a minute or two at first, then allow it to grow into more.

3. **Invite** Jesus to be with you. I use a modified version of the prayer of St. Patrick to help center my heart's affections and my mind's thoughts, but you can develop your own focused prayer, whatever is comfortable for you.

Christ above me, very God of very God
Christ below me, incarnate of the earth
Christ before me when I see
Christ behind me when I cannot see
Christ at my right hand in my strength
Christ at me left in my weakness
Christ in me, the hope of glory, formed by faith

4. **Read** the <u>entire</u> scripture passage for that day. Don't skim. As a Pastor and teacher, I believe at my core that context is everything, and we do ourselves a disservice by pulling random scriptures and trying to apply them apart from their context. There is a key verse for each day, but I have tried to structure the readings in such a way that you will gain at least some of the context present.

5. **Reflect** on the passage and devotional reading. Give yourself time to do this.

6. **Pray.** A short prayer is included at the end of each day's reading and is designed to be a starting point. Ask the Lord to speak into your heart the things he wants you to pray from the day's reading.

7. **Journal.** This is a difficult practice for some and life-giving for others. I encourage you to at least try this practice, as it will help you process what God is saying to you in this season and give you a way to look back on your journey.

The 46 days in this devotional begin with Ash Wednesday and culminate with Holy Saturday. Why 46 days? Sundays have always been considered sacred days of celebration for Christians and, therefore, are not included in the 40-day fasting practice. When Sundays are added into equation, the 46 days are complete. In this Lenten season, may you capture the awe, joy, and wonder of Christ as we journey to the cross.

Grace to you all.

Jon Jennings (Glendale, AZ 2023)

JOURNEY
TO THE CROSS
A REFLECTIVE LENTEN DEVOTIONAL

FIRST DAY OF LENT
ASH WEDNESDAY
"THE FELLOWSHIP"

Reading: Philippians 3:7-20

My goal is to know him and the power of his resurrection and the fellowship of his sufferings, being conformed to his death.

PHILIPPIANS 3:10 (CSB)

FOR MILLIONS OF CHRISTIANS across the world, today marks the official beginning of the 46-day period of prayer and fasting leading to Easter. These are not days of isolation, but rather days of engagement. As we journey with Christ through the final season of His time on Earth, we seek to experience key moments with our Savior that happened along the way to Jerusalem.

This experience, however, is not one of a passive observer. It requires commitment and action. At the end of his letter to the Philippians, Paul speaks of actively pursuing knowledge of Christ in three areas:

- The power of His resurrection
- The fellowship of His sufferings
- Conforming to His death

By pursuing these things, His journey becomes our journey. Seeking to know Him surpasses the incongruity of knowing Him in our minds, but not in our actions. Both are necessary, and all else is rubbish when compared to a life actively joined to Christ. Pursuing this, we experience all that He is and all that He does.

Actively following Christ over the next 46 days invites us to engage our senses in a tangible way. We see, hear, smell, taste, and touch not only who He is, but also what He does. It has less to do with how we feel about Jesus, and more to do with how we experience Him in our thoughts and actions. In this season, we seek to know Him by reaching forward to what is ahead, pressing toward the goal of solidarity with the Savior.

We experience the power of His resurrection, knowing death is defeated, and God is restoring the world one life at a time. The power of God works in us and through us in a tangible way as we invite the Savior of the world to intersect every dark, depressed, and distressed life, seeking to infuse them with His saving grace.

We experience the fellowship of His suffering knowing the Savior's suffering was not to appease an angry, wrathful God, but rather to join us in our suffering. Through His suffering, Christ became our peace, breaking down the barriers which keep humanity from God; and by knowing Him, we make a conscious decision to do the same. When we actively engage in the world, we too are joined in solidarity with a suffering world. During this period of Lent, we journey to His cross while bearing the cross we have taken up to follow the lead of the Messiah. This brings us to the last experience – being conformed to His death.

Conformed means "having the same likeness." We are not being asked to die, but we seek to be like Him in action and attitude. Every circumstance may be different, but to be conformed to His death means we accept what God intends in those circumstances regardless of the consequences. We seek out and accept the Father's plan for our lives, not with despair, but with hope, recognizing death is not the end, but a means to the ultimate hope of eternal life. Through the Lenten season, this is the life we choose – an experience – a journey which brings us into oneness with Christ.

Father, through this season of Lent, may I truly come to know you in a deeper way. Allow this season to be a time where I experience you and actively participate with you in the power of your resurrection, and fellowship of your suffering. May I always seek to conform my life to your will regardless of the personal discomfort it may bring. I realize that a higher purpose is at work through every circumstance, and may I rejoice with hope, knowing you have my best interest at heart. In Christ's name, amen.

SECOND DAY OF LENT
THURSDAY
"THE CONFESSION"

Reading: Matthew 16:13-20

Simon Peter answered, "You are the Messiah, the Son of the living God."

MATTHEW 16:16 (CSB)

NEAR THE BASE OF MT. HERMON in Northern Israel stand the ancient ruins of Caesarea Philippi. Once home to a pagan shrine, the site was built by Herod's son, Phillip, in the early 1st century. The shrine once boasted a temple dedicated to Augustus, first Caesar of Rome, another to the Greek god, Zeus, and a massive courtyard where the pagans worshiped Pan, the god of fright (think panic). The massive rock formation behind this pagan playground contains a large cave which the ancients believed to be the gateway to the underworld, the place of the gods. It is no accident Jesus chose this location to pose a question to His closest followers about His identity.

"Who do people say I am?

"What's the word on the street about me?"

The rock of Caesarea Philippi also has hewn niches which, in the time of Jesus, held statues dedicated to the Greek gods of the day including Pan's father, Hermes and his cohort, Echo, among others. As the disciples gave Jesus the word from the street – "you are Elijah, Jeremiah, John the Baptist, or one of the prophets," Jesus compelled the disciples to answer for themselves.

"Among the pantheon of gods represented here at this pagan site – among the opinions of men, what do you say? Who am I?"

All of us must answer this question for ourselves because the situation is the same today. The word on our 21st century streets will vary as to who Jesus is. Some will call Him a great teacher, a great prophet, or just another person who did good for all. Yet, Peter's answer, "you are the Messiah, the Son of the living God" was a revelation from heaven and remains the answer.

The Messiah, the Chosen One, came to reveal God to humanity and to do His will in a unique way. Those who confess this truth become part of a movement, the church, tasked with expanding God's Kingdom on Earth. The church Jesus said He would build on this confession should never be reduced to a physical edifice or stationary group of passive spectators. The church is an assembly of people who follow The Way of Jesus and are called to advance His Way across all generations.

By coming to Earth, Jesus re-established the rule and reign of God and His invitation to all is to filter out the noise of the word on the street about Him. We are challenged to separate Him from the pantheon of gods permeating our culture, including the god of self, and to simply follow Him.

This moment at Caesarea Philippi was a pivotal moment for both Jesus and the disciples. The popular Galilean ministry the disciples enjoyed was full of massive crowds and undeniable miracles, but it was now behind them, and the focus of our Lord was turned toward Jerusalem. While Jesus always knew His mission, the journey to the cross begins here in Caesarea Philippi. The disciples failed to understand what we often fail to understand. The journey to the cross for Jesus is also our journey, for this journey defines true discipleship and what it really means to follow the one who is the Messiah, the Son of the living God.

Father, as I begin this journey, open my mouth to boldly and unashamedly confess among all opinions that you are indeed the Messiah, the Son of the living God. Open my eyes to see what you are calling me to - a life of discipleship that seeks to follow your way. Open my ears to hear your voice as you reveal my shortcomings and challenge me to a new level of discipleship. Allow me to taste and touch the Divine this season. In Christ's name, amen.

THIRD DAY OF LENT
FRIDAY
INTERLUDE -THE FIRST PREDICTION OF JESUS' DEATH

From then on Jesus began to point out to his disciples that it was necessary for him to go to Jerusalem and suffer many things from the elders, chief priests, and scribes, be killed, and be raised the third day. Peter took him aside and began to rebuke him, "Oh no, Lord! This will never happen to you!" Jesus turned and told Peter, "Get behind me, Satan! You are a hindrance to me because you're not thinking about God's concerns but human concerns."

MATTHEW 16:21-23 (NAS)

THE SHIFT FROM POPULAR MINISTRY to the journey to the cross has begun. For the disciples, confessing Christ as the Messiah was only the first step. Now, Jesus moves them into a season of deep preparation and makes it clear the upcoming journey is necessary. It is necessary for Him to go to Jerusalem. It is necessary for Him to suffer, die, and be raised again. Peter, however, didn't see it that way and by taking Jesus aside, he crossed a line that effectively put him in league with the work of Satan. "Lord, this will never happen to you!" In essence, Peter wanted the Kingdom without the cross and before we criticize the one who confessed Christ as the Son of God, let us examine our own lives while considering this exchange between Jesus and Peter.

The reason Jesus called Peter, "Satan," is because of what happened in the wilderness temptation (see Matthew 4). In the wilderness, Satan offered Jesus both popularity and greatness. Based on what Peter had seen in his time with Jesus, he believed the miraculous demonstrations of the Galilean ministry needed to continue. Peter's limited understanding defined success by temporal measures. Jesus, however, had a completely different definition of success, to embrace suffering and failure as a primary mark of discipleship. Jesus knew what Peter didn't know and what we often lose sight of: Success is doing God's will, God's way, in God's timing. "Peter," Jesus said, "you aren't thinking about God's concerns – only human concerns. I am concerned about the eternal. You are concerned with the here and now."

Peter, like Satan, became a hindrance (stumbling block) to Jesus fulfilling His mission. The word "hindrance" literally means "the trigger of a trap" and in this powerful discipleship moment, our Lord tells Peter he is unknowingly trying to lure Him into the same traps the devil laid out in the wilderness. Peter's thinking must be reshaped as must ours. Throughout this journey, let us allow Jesus to redefine our thoughts and what success means considering the cross. It may not be the popular way, but it is the Jesus Way.

Father, today I take stock of how I have defined success. Forgive me for pursuing success as defined by the world, with power, prestige, and possessions. Refocus my mind toward your definition of success, which is to do your will, your way, in your timing regardless of the hardships involved. Give me the grace by your Spirit to avoid the traps Satan sets to draw me away from your purpose. In Christ's name, amen.

———————————————————

FOURTH DAY OF LENT
SATURDAY
"THE BEST LIFE"

Reading: Matthew 16:24-28

Then Jesus said to his disciples, "If anyone wants to follow after me, let him deny himself, take up his cross, and follow me.

MATTHEW 16:24 (CSB)

I LOVE FLYING. No, I'm not crazy about being stuck in a large, hollow, hot metal tube for hours competing for elbow space on the arm rest with the person next to me. What I love most about flying is the take off. I love…

The thrust and roar of the jet engines,
The acceleration down the runway,
The flaps of the wings down and…

Within seconds…lift off!

The ground beneath no longer holds, and we are soaring through the clouds to our destination praying our luggage makes it at the same time we do.

The call by Jesus to His disciples as the journey to the cross begins involves lift off. "Take up your cross" means "to lift from the ground – to lift in order to carry off." This powerful act that on the surface, sounds like a hard-knock life is quite the opposite. It is our best life. Human nature strives on its own power and strength to live the best possible life. We pursue the consumeristic notion of the "American Dream" or the "Western Dream" with the hope of acquiring enough possessions to live comfortably and securely. While there is nothing inherently wrong with this quest, it is the constant pursuit of self-indulgence and self-satisfaction which robs us of the best possible life.

"Take up" is seen in Exodus 34:6-7 as God forgiving and removing the burden of sin from us.

The LORD — the LORD is a compassionate and gracious God, slow to anger and abounding in faithful love and truth, maintaining faithful love to a thousand generations, forgiving iniquity, rebellion, and sin... (Exodus 34:6-7a CSB emphasis added)

He "takes up" our sin and invites us to come under the covering of His life and ways. When we take up our cross as a disciple of Jesus, we place ourselves under His canopy of life and by living His way, we have the capacity to soar to heights unimaginable. Is His way easy? In one sense, yes. His yoke is easy, and His burden is light. But in another sense, it is difficult because it involves a willingness to deny ourselves, and all it entails. When we take up our cross, our identities, desires, goals, dreams, and pursuits become His. For the closest disciples of Jesus, they had left everything to follow Him – businesses, families, and communities. Now, the commitment to follow goes to a new level. Deny yourself. Take up your cross.

When we deny ourselves, we effectively reverse what happened in the Garden of Eden. The serpent told Eve to decide for herself what was right and good and not allow God to deprive her of good fruit from a great tree. In that moment of decision, it was no longer about the truth of what God said, but what Eve decided about what God said. It was an outright rejection of God's truth, replaced with her own version of the truth. Reflecting upon this great reversal, I realize I am bent in the same direction as Eve, and while I want to self-evaluate and make my own determination of what God said, I must opt for His truth no matter what. Then, my life is aligned with Him, and only then can I truly say I am following Him.

This is what losing our own lives and finding His is all about. I give up the blueprint I formerly used for my life and replace it with Christ's blueprint for my life. Yes, the cross is suffering and hardship, but it demonstrates the greatest measure of perfect love – self-giving, radically forgiving, sacrificial love. When I deny myself, take up my cross and follow, I lose my life, but I gain His. That is truly the best life.

Father, forgive me for trying to do life on my own. I recognize I am selfishly bent toward my own wants and desires yet these efforts to find my best life have still left me wanting. Today, I choose your way. I choose to take up my cross and come underneath it, carrying it as a blessed canopy of your love. Allow me to live in a way that always says yes to you no matter what. I truly desire your life which is the best life. In Christ's name, amen.

FIRST SUNDAY OF LENT

"THE TRANSFIGURATION"

Reading: Luke 9:28-36

As He was praying, the appearance (countenance) of His face changed...a cloud appeared...they entered the cloud. Then a voice came from the cloud, saying "This is my Son, the chosen one; listen to Him."

LUKE 9:29-35 (CSB - PARENTHESES ADDED)

WHEN MY YOUNGEST DAUGHTER CHARITY was about 6 years old, I started praying the blessing of Aaron over her at night before she went to bed. Early on in this tradition, she would smile brightly, and her face would radiate as if the words of the blessing were happening in real time. Even when I traveled, I would either call her at night or send her a picture of this incredible blessing and our tradition went on for about ten years. Even now, at age 17, I will speak this over her life, as it is such a powerful reminder of what God desires to do for us through His Son.

The LORD bless you and keep you; the LORD make his face to shine upon you and be gracious to you; the LORD lift up his countenance upon you and give you peace.
(Numbers 6:24-26 ESV)

About a week after the turning point at Caesarea Philippi, Jesus, along with Peter, James, and John went to a high mountain to pray. Weary from the climb, the disciples fell asleep, but once awakened, they became participants in a miraculous event. This multi-layered experience, known as the transfiguration, gives us insight into many things such as Christ's voice being the fulfillment of the law and the prophets and the future glory of the Father resting upon the Son. There are other emphases made by Luke in this story which warrant our attention.

When Moses and Elijah appeared on the mountain with Jesus, they spoke of His departure that would soon be brought to completion in Jerusalem. "Departure" is "exodus" in the original language and Luke makes it clear to his readers that Jesus and His cross-centered mission will become a new exodus for humanity. The exodus was the defining moment for Israel hastening a departure from the slavery and servitude of Egypt into a land of freedom, hope and promise. When God's people passed through the waters of the Red Sea, the exodus signaled a passing from death unto life. For us, the exodus is a redeeming work for all humanity as Christ, the Passover Lamb, has made the way for us to pass through from death unto life. The cross, thus, provides an exodus from a life of bondage to sin into a new life of freedom and victory.

As the three disciples were roused from sleep, Peter wanted to build three shelters or tabernacles, connecting the transfiguration event to the Jewish Feast of Tabernacles (Sukkot) which would soon be celebrated on the journey to the cross. Sukkot commemorated the journey of Israel in the wilderness after the exodus, and now Jesus, the Passover Lamb, stands as the fulfillment of Sukkot as well. But let's not miss the point: The soon to be accomplished departure of Jesus has everything to do with His redemptive work. All road signs now pointed to one place – Jerusalem. The sum of Christ's purpose for coming to Earth will soon be fulfilled.

Moses and Elijah, the law, and the prophets, now give way to the Son of God who is the New Exodus. As we journey to the cross, we are challenged to experience our own exodus and make the radical departure from the old to the new. Only through His Exodus can we experience the exodus. We listen to the Chosen One, the Son of God. For in Him, all things are fulfilled, and this is when the Lord's face shines brightly upon our lives, His countenance is lifted upon us, and He gives us His peace. Our countenance is then changed, transfigured, and we reflect God's glory to the world, experiencing His Exodus in real time.

Father, I desire above all things to live a life that reflects you. Awaken my soul to the reality that you, my Exodus, forged a path for my exodus from death unto life. Allow each breath I take to inhale the wonder of your glory, and with each breath that is exhaled in this world bring glory to you. In Christ's name, amen.

FIFTH DAY OF LENT
MONDAY
"THE UNBELIEF"

Reading: Mark 9:14-29

Immediately, the father of the boy cried out, "I do believe.
Help my unbelief."

MARK 9:24 (CSB)

THE FATHER IN THIS STORY IS ME. It's you. It's all of us. As a father of 5, I may not know what it's like to have a demon-possessed child, but I certainly know what it's like to have a sick child. I have spent many sleepless nights at the bedside of my children who were afflicted by illness, watching with vigilance to make sure they were still breathing. I have walked the floor with them cradled in my arms. I have spent countless hours praying and singing over them, begging God to intervene on their behalf. I have pushed back the tears in hospital rooms as my child lay helplessly stretched out with IV's and oxygen tubes, all-the-while fighting the urge to be angry with God for observing from heaven and doing nothing.

As a Pastor, I have prayed over congregants for healings, financial miracles, wayward children, addiction, trauma, deliverance, and revival of spirit. There have been times I have seen God intervene instantly. At other times, a slow process of Divine intervention ensued while at other times, God seemingly did nothing, and the situation remained the same.

Lord, I do believe. Help my unbelief.

Most of us, like the father with the demon-possessed son, vacillate between belief and unbelief. We know God can, but we are just not certain He will. Ironically, faith and doubt are not merely cognitive exercises which take place only in the mind. Unbelief means "unfaithfulness" which is an action, not a thought. Faith apart from action is dead (see James 1) if it only exists in our mind. Faith's action is trust in a person, the person of Jesus, and I cannot say I have faith if I cannot put the entire weight of my life and my circumstances upon Him.

This is what the father in the story is doing. He positions his life before the Son of God saying, "here I am, believing. Here I am, standing before you ready to do whatever it takes. I trust you based on what I know. You have proven yourself!" But then, the father admits his lack. "I know you can. I don't know if you will. I have lived this demonic reality with my son for years and even your own disciples could do nothing about it. This situation is real and undeniable. I do believe. Help my unbelief."

This man knew in his mind Jesus could bring deliverance and deep down, he desired to give total trust. He just didn't know how. That's where some of you are. You have heard the words of hope that God is good, able, and willing to help. You desperately believe your circumstances can change, but you have been disappointed too many times. You feel like it's your fault and somehow if you could supernaturally conjure up a little more faith, you could move the hand of God.

The key for us is to follow this desperate father's lead. Stand before the Lord, fully trusting who He is, then simply offer ourselves. I believe. Here I stand. I'm not perfect but accept what I can offer as enough. Help my unbelief. My perspective is flawed and far from perfect. I am willing, but I just need help. Jesus, fresh off the Mount of Transfiguration, saw the vulnerability and honesty of this desperate father, and it was enough. The healing came, and that is all Jesus really wants from us – trust, vulnerability, and honesty. I do believe. Help my unbelief.

Father, when situations get desperate, I admit I have no answers outside of you. Forgive me for taking on a posture which minimizes your ability to do all things and grant me the grace to simply trust and offer the only thing I really have – myself. Allow me to rest in your goodness and be transparent enough to admit when my faith is struggling. Lord, I do believe, but help my unbelief. In Christ's name, amen.

SIXTH DAY OF LENT
TUESDAY
INTERLUDE -THE SECOND PREDICTION OF JESUS' DEATH

Then they left that place and made their way through Galilee, but he did not want anyone to know it. For he was teaching his disciples and telling them, "The Son of Man is going to be betrayed into the hands of men. They will kill him, and after he is killed, he will rise three days later." But they did not understand this statement, and they were afraid to ask him.

MATTHEW 9:30-32 (CSB)

THERE ARE MOMENTS WHEN FOLLOWING JESUS, we are drawn aside, special moments when our Lord takes us deeper in our discipleship and teaches us greater truths concerning His Kingdom. In some cases, it feels like one-on-one tutoring, as the Master Teacher imparts details about things difficult to grasp.

For a second time, Jesus predicts His passion to the 12, yet the idea of suffering, death, and resurrection remains elusive. They didn't understand and we too are like this. Jesus draws us aside to challenge us or show us His plan for our life, but because of our own ideals of what we think He wants to do, we inadvertently block off our ability to grasp the new thing Christ wants to do, especially if the way involves hardship and difficulty.

As the group passed through Galilee moving toward Jerusalem, no doubt the disciples recalled the amazing miracles and teaching that took place in that region early on. It was a great time for the 12 as they left everything and launched into a season of following this amazing man of God. There is a vast difference, however, between "come and follow" and "come and die." Every season of life has its unique purpose and the journey to the cross will prove to be a time of even deeper following, learning, and suffering.

In this moment, we set aside our preconceived notions of what God may be doing in our lives and lean into His understanding rather than our own. The disciples confessed Him as Lord in Caesarea Philippi and learned to hear His voice on the Mount of Transfiguration. Now they must learn the ways of the Kingdom at a new level. The journey to the cross continues.

Father, I have chosen to follow you. Regardless of what my expectations were in the beginning of my journey with you, I recognize each season has a purpose. There will be seasons of great joy and seasons of great sorrow. Show me how to walk through every season with consistency and fervor. Difficult times present a powerful opportunity for growth, and I resolve this day to walk with you in the power of your Spirit to learn what I need for the next phase of the journey. In Christ's name, amen.

Reading: Mark 9:33-42

"OWN YOUR OWN STUFF!" That is how we raised our kids, and this phrase hasn't always been a gentle encouragement in our home but rather, a challenge. Jennings don't blame-shift or look for scapegoats. When we create messes, make mistakes, or leave others in the wake of our destruction, we own our stuff. Such is the way of the Kingdom and the lifestyle of a true Jesus-follower.

The journey of Jesus and the disciples through Galilee stops in their home base of Capernaum. This beautiful town on the north shore of the lake was an important place for Jesus to anchor His ministry, as it lay on a major trade route at the intersection of three major political regions. The local economy was built around two industries: fishing and milling. At least four of the 12 disciples came from Capernaum as fishermen, but Jesus chose the milling industry to illustrate one of the greatest, yet most misunderstood principles of discipleship.

Paused in the bustling Galilean town, Jesus taught His followers what true greatness looks like. He expounded on what it means to treat children with dignity and honor, and extend welcome to those who follow Jesus, but may not be part of the inner circle. Then Jesus makes this statement.

> But whoever causes one of these little ones who believe in me to fall away – it would be better for him if a heavy millstone were hung around his neck and he were thrown into the sea
> (Mark 9:42 CSB)

Some translations of "fall away" read "to stumble." "Whoever causes another disciple to stumble or fall away from the faith, it would be better…" The imagery here is bold, and in your face, given the Capernaum context. A millstone was a large wheel-shaped stone used for grinding grain. It was so heavy, weighing hundreds of pounds, a beast of burden was used to move and turn it. Jesus said it would be better to have one of these around your neck and be thrown into Galilee than to be the cause of someone falling away, stumbling, or tripping away from Jesus. Perhaps we read this and default to thinking about our own lifestyle. Rightly so.

Actions speak louder than words and we must always ask if our lives are being lived out in such a way it reflects Christ to the world. Own your stuff. Deal with your own sins and shortcomings because one thing our generation can sniff out in a heartbeat is hypocrisy, an incongruent life which speaks one thing and lives another.

There is another aspect of causing others to fall which demands attention. If I see another disciple of Christ falling into a trap, or if they are near a stumbling block, I have an obligation to warn them. Speaking truth in love, I owe it to my brothers and sisters to help them see their blind spots. I would want someone to do this for me, but somehow when the tables are turned, we are afraid to offend and we back away.

Following Jesus is the most important life one can choose, and God forbid we should ever be the cause of someone's stumbling either by our own actions, or a failure to lovingly spare someone else from their own ruin. That is a weight of millstone proportions I don't want to carry. Let's own our own stuff and help others to do the same. We need partners for the journey, not millstones to carry around our necks.

Father, there are moments in life I need to take inventory. Does my life truly reflect you? Do my actions match my words? But there is another task with this inventory I bring before you today. Do I watch out for my brothers and sisters in the faith? Do I come along side to help them see their blind spots, not in a judgmental way, but in a way which truly desires their best interests? I pause today and ask these questions in humility before you. Reveal truth to me by your Holy Spirit. In Christ's name, amen.

EIGHTH DAY OF LENT
THURSDAY
"THE UNFORGIVING SERVANT"

Reading: Matthew 18:21-34

Shouldn't you also have had mercy on your fellow servant, as I had mercy on you?

MATTHEW 18:33 (CSB)

IN THE WINTER OF 2008, we took a family ski adventure to the White Mountains in Eastern Arizona. Our 15-year-old son, Chris, decided to try snowboarding for the first time on this trip. While coming down the mountain on a run, his board caught an edge and he took a serious fall – so serious, in fact, he had to be transported to a nearby hospital for head injury treatment. Fortunately, it was only a mild concussion, but it could have been far worse.

Obtaining medical treatment in the U.S. can be a costly endeavor, as much of the incurred expense is passed on to the patient, unlike other places in the world. A few weeks after we arrived home, we received a bill from the hospital. It was an astronomical amount, more than we could afford to pay at the time. I decided to throw myself at the mercy of our creditors and work out a plan where we could pay the debt over time. The hospital placed me on hold for what seemed like an eternity and when the agent came back on the phone, she delivered news that nearly sent me into shock. "Mr. Jennings, we have determined that you owe us nothing." The elation that swept over me in that moment is something I will never forget.

"You don't owe me."

That is forgiveness. In this parable, Jesus told a powerful story of a servant who was forgiven by a king of an unpayable debt yet refused to extend that same forgiveness to one who owed him a minuscule amount. The king who extended the forgiveness was enraged, calling the servant "wicked" and laying out in the clearest possible terms what should have happened. "You should have given the same mercy you received."

Life in God's Kingdom has no room for unforgiveness. Earlier in this conversation, Peter tried to put a limit on the number of times we must forgive those who wrong us. Jesus didn't take the bait. In His Kingdom there is no measure on forgiveness. When we said "yes" to Jesus, repented of our old life, and committed to living His way, the powerful words "I forgive you" were declared over us by our Savior. Jesus says to all who turn to Him in faith, "You don't owe me." We entered into the Kingdom with a zero balance, a clean slate all because Christ paid a debt He did not owe for all who owed a debt they could not pay. This is where the challenge comes in.

We who have been forgiven are now obligated to extend the forgiveness we have received. We demonstrate we have been forgiven by living and acting in accordance with that same forgiveness. I have found in my own life if I truly honor my King, my life will reflect His generosity on every level, including a refusal to hold grudges and harbor unforgiveness. This is one way we can all excel in the mission of bringing the Kingdom of God to Earth.

Forgiveness does not excuse the wrong done to us, nor does it guarantee reconciliation. Forgiveness does release the person to Christ and rolls our burdens of pain, hurt, and trauma onto Him, opening the door for healing to come to our own heart. It all begins with the powerful words, "I forgive you. You don't owe me." Would we rather release all to Jesus, or remain in our own dark place of torment for the wrongs done to us? I choose the former. "You don't owe me."

Father, I am forever grateful of the forgiveness and mercy you have extended to me. I did nothing to deserve it, but you gave it freely. I pray today that I would always stay in this posture of forgiveness toward others. When I am wronged by others, do not allow bitterness and unforgiveness to lodge in my heart. Remind me of what I have freely received and allow me to freely give this gift of forgiveness. In Christ's name, amen.

NINTH DAY OF LENT
FRIDAY
"THE LONG GAME"

Reading: Luke 9:51-56

But he turned and rebuked them, and they went to another village.

LUKE 9:55-56 (CSB)

IN OUR FAST-PACED, instant gratification world, we often lack the patience to play the long game. Think in terms of personal finance. To plan well for the future, we must spend less than we make, save, invest well, and be patient through rocky economic cycles. The short game says, "buy the 85-inch TV and the car that will pinch your budget now." The long game is always about patience and trusting the process.

The long game principles apply in other areas of life – sports, personal health, relationships, etc… but rarely do we consider the long game as it relates to God's Kingdom. We want our blessing now. We want our miracle now. We want to become Christ-like now. Jesus was fully committed to the long game, and we see this vividly portrayed in this interaction with His disciples concerning a Samaritan village.

When the journey to Jerusalem commenced, Jesus was resolute in His purpose and mission. Advance planning and preparation were necessary for such a trip. When a Samaritan village refused hospitality for the traveling band, the Brothers Zebedee (let's call them the Bee Zees) wanted to do what Elijah did in Samaria centuries earlier – call fire from heaven and wipe them off the map. After all, the Jews and Samaritans had a very rocky relational history with no love lost between them. Surely God would be open to a repeat performance!

Violence, however, is never the way of the Kingdom and the church throughout history has not quite figured this out. Taking up arms, blowing up buildings, and inciting the masses with hate-filled diatribes is the short game which may bring instant gratification, but tarnishes the witness of Jesus in a world that needs a demonstration of His mercy and grace. Jesus had a plan for Samaria to hear and receive the good news, but it was the long game.

For Jesus, the long game started with a Samaritan woman who received Jesus as a life-giving prophet and testified to her village, making the Samaritan field "white unto harvest" (John 4). When our Lord healed 10 lepers on the journey to the cross (Luke 17), the one who turned and gave thanks was a Samaritan. And who can forget the powerful story of a Samaritan who provided healing, care, and financial resources for a man left to die on the road to Jericho (Luke 10)? Interacting with Samaritans and recognizing their examples of gratitude and graciousness was part of Jesus' long game.

After Christ's ascension, one of His followers, Philip, went to Samaria and preached the gospel in many villages with signs following (Acts 8). Revival was sparked, but the groundwork was laid much earlier as Jesus played the long game. Today's world needs the gospel and we, the people of God, cannot be afraid of the long game. When James and John wanted to play the short game, the way of violence and retribution, Jesus rebuked them and told them they were operating out of the wrong spirit. The right spirit requires patience.

Not everyone will receive the message of the Kingdom or embrace the way of Jesus, but we do not stop planting seed or proclaiming the truth. Let's be honest, the world at times sees an angry, hateful, vengeance-driven people representing the one who modeled the opposite. We need a different game, His game, the long game. Maybe we should simply shake off the dust and move on to another village.

Father, I realize we as your people need to see the world through your eyes. Our vision is limited, and our perspective is often flawed. Forgive us for the times we have been short-sighted and acted impulsively toward others rather than discerning your will and purpose for the moment, and for their lives. Give us the capacity to slow down, allow the Spirit to work the fruit of patience in us so we can play the long game. In Christ's name, amen.

TENTH DAY OF LENT
SATURDAY
"THE TIME"

Reading: John 7:1-14

Jesus told them, "My time has not yet arrived, but your time is always at hand."

JOHN 7:6 (CSB)

IN SCHOOL, I WAS A CLOCK-WATCHER. These were old school clocks with hands moving slowly along counting the human measurement of time. By watching the clock, I could predict with relative ease the precise moment when the second hand would sweep across a given point on the face, and the bell would ring. In the ancient past, civilizations measured time by the solar day (amounts of light and darkness), the lunar month (following the phases of the moon as it rotates around the Earth), and the solar year (defined by the changing of the seasons as the Earth revolves around the sun.)

Ancient measurements and sophisticated mechanical clocks have given way to atomic clocks delivering unparalleled accuracy to the 100-quadrillionth of a second. The bottom line: human beings measure time in linear fashion. Seconds make up minutes which turn into hours, which grow into days, and evolve into years. We are conditioned to live by our calendars with alerts set to remind of our commitments to temporal measurements of time. God does not operate like this. He is not bound by human measurements of time. He transcends time.

The New Testament uses two words for time: "chronos" (chronological time) and "kairos" (a time that is set by God). Think of it this way: kairos is a fixed moment, determined by God as He intersects and intervenes in the chronos. Still confused? We march through time clicking off the minutes, hours, days, weeks, and years. God can, and does, show up in His time to reveal His purpose in any given situation. Kairos moments are the times in our lives God has set and appointed to fulfill and advance His Kingdom in us and through us.

Jesus fully understood this. When His brothers, who were not believers at the time, pushed Him to go to a major feast in Jerusalem to publicly display His miracle-working power, Jesus had a simple response. "My time (kairos), my fixed moment, has not yet arrived." From a natural perspective, Jesus' brothers made perfect sense. "If you really want to be recognized and become an influencer widening the top of your funnel, go to Jerusalem now. Show yourself to the world! This is a great opportunity for you to build your brand." "No," Jesus said. "My God-appointed moment isn't here – yet." A few days later, Jesus indeed went to the festival not to reveal Himself as His brothers wished, but rather, to teach. Jesus' destiny,

His kairos, was the cross and it would all be accomplished in the chronos when God decided the kairos.

So many of us are waiting for God to intervene. We long for a kairos moment when God's sovereignty intersects our faith. Circumstances which need His intervention long for such moments, but may we never fall into the trap of Jesus' brothers whose understanding was clouded by unbelief. Kairos moments generally happen behind the scenes of an ordinary day when opposition wars against our soul. In those moments, we remain steadfast in our faith, keeping our eyes fixed on the One who holds the chronos in His hands. Jesus' response to His brothers speaks volumes.

> "...your time (kairos) is always at hand."
> (John 7:6 CSB parentheses added)

Jesus was saying, "the God-appointed time for you to believe and put your faith in me is always there." Every moment for us is a kairos moment. As we wait for His appointed time to arrive, we seize our own kairos moment, placing all our confidence and faith in Him. Our time is always at hand. We can stop watching the clock now.

Father, I admit that my connection to temporal time has unintentionally eroded my faith and confidence in you. Often, it is hard for me to grasp the way you operate when it comes to intervening in life situations. Today is a new day with new mercies, and I choose to lean into the mercies of this new day to give my faith opportunity to grow. Remind me that you hold all things in your hands, and you will indeed show up in your appointed kairos moment. In Christ's name, amen.

SECOND SUNDAY OF LENT

"THE RIVER"

Reading: John 7:37-44

"He who believes in Me, as the Scripture has said, out of his heart will flow rivers of living water."

JOHN 7:38 (NKJ)

IT IS THE FALL OF THE YEAR in Jerusalem when Jesus arrives for the festival. The Jews know it as Sukkot, the Feast of Tabernacles, one of three pilgrimage feasts for God's people alongside Passover and Pentecost. Make-shift huts, or booths were sprayed across the hills outside the old city, and for eight days, the pilgrims commemorated the 40 years of wandering in the wilderness after the exodus. It was a celebration of deliverance, recalling of God's faithfulness, provision, and compassion. The days of the festival were filled with eating, dancing, leaping for joy, and thanksgiving to a God who had redeemed, is redeeming, and will continue to redeem His people. Past, present, and future hope all come together as one in this great feast.

The festivities of Sukkot included a daily water ceremony. Water was drawn from the Pool of Siloam south of the city and carried up the steep slope to the courtyard of the temple where it was then poured out upon the altar. As the water was poured out, the people sang from the Psalms, particularly Psalm 118. Words from the prophets Zechariah and Ezekiel were read aloud.

> On that day, living water will flow out from Jerusalem.
> (Zechariah 14:8 CSB)

> Since the water will become fresh, there will be life
> everywhere the river goes.
> (Ezekiel 47:9 CSB)

While the prophets may have envisioned an actual river flowing at the end of days, Jesus sees a different kind of river flowing as He prepares to finish His earthly work. He sees a river flowing from Himself as the Chief Cornerstone of God's temple. On this great day of the feast, Jesus declared to the masses that all who are truly thirsty for life-giving, life-changing water need look no further. Their search was over, and they could come to Him and drink.

With echoes from the conversation with the Samaritan woman (John 4), John brilliantly connects the dots for us. Christ alone is living water. This life-giving water, however, does not become like the Dead Sea which has no outlet. Those who have believed and placed the entire weight of their lives on Jesus will also receive His Spirit and as a result, the same life which is in Him will come to us and flow from us to bring healing to the nations.

The same Spirit which hovered over the waters of creation and brought order out of chaos is the same Spirit now available to us. Our world is in chaos, and desperately needs the people of God to step in, and with a Spirit-infused, life-giving, refreshing way, bring God's order to our chaotic world. We rejoice and celebrate with thanksgiving on this day because with joy, we have drawn our water from the wells of salvation and invited the rivers of living water to come forth.

Father, we know when the world is at its worst, it needs the people of God at their best. We honor you best when your life is coming from us as a river to the parched, dry ground of our world. People are thirsty for real, living water and your Son, Jesus, gives us the perfect well from which to draw. We choose to draw from that well this day and may the same refreshing that has come to us through Jesus flow from us to bring healing to the nations. In Christ's name, amen.

ELEVENTH DAY OF LENT
MONDAY
"THE ACCUSERS"

Reading: John 8:2-11

When Jesus had raised Himself up and saw no one but the woman, He said to her, "Woman, where are those accusers of yours? Has no one condemned you?"

JOHN 8:10 (NKJ)

I GUESS THE RULES DON'T APPLY TO ME! I have uttered that statement out loud more than once, not about myself, mind you. No, it's never about me. It's about others who try and skirt the system by creating a set of standards which only apply to them. Case in point, the school pickup line.

When my kids were in elementary school, the school administrators issued clear instructions for the afternoon pickup, which was logistically far worse than the morning drop off. These instructions included where to queue up, which lane to use, where to park, and where not to park. Without fail, parents tried to find workarounds to pick up their kids and avoid the mayhem. Usually, these workarounds included parking in the middle of lanes, blocking other cars, and inevitably slowing down the entire process. Never mind that on more than one occasion, the violating vehicle sported one of our church stickers on its rear window. In these moments, with my own windows rolled up, the phrase echoed in my car – "I guess the rules don't apply to me!" Keeping it real, there may have been a time or two when I made my own pickup rules, but I will neither confirm, nor deny.

This redeeming story from John, situated around the time of Sukkot, is a beautiful picture dispelling the myth that the rules don't apply to us. Normally when this story is read, the focus is on Christ extending mercy to a woman accused of what was a capital crime under the system of her day, adultery. This merciful focus is right, for Jesus not only frees the woman from condemnation, He also releases her to accept His invitation and live her life in the freedom of God's ways where sin is no longer a primary practice.

For the woman's accusers, there is an equally powerful message. Under the Torah, no person could stand condemned of breaking the law unless two or three witnesses verified the accusation, but here is the twist. If the accusers were proven false, violating the eighth commandment about bearing false witness against a neighbor, their fate would be the same as if they were the accused. Thus, bearing false witness against this woman would become a capital crime. No witness would want that fate which explains why the accusers slithered away as Jesus wrote in the ground.

Whatever Jesus wrote in the ground, His point was made. The rules apply to everyone no matter what sticker is on your car. Bearing false witness against our neighbor is a serious thing and in our modern culture, such behavior is commonplace. As God's people, we hold ourselves to a higher standard, recognizing our own flaws, and refusing to cast stones.

Our journey to the cross reminds us of what Jesus truly came to do. He died to destroy the works of the devil and while Jesus never gave the woman in the story a free pass, He did raise the bar of discipleship. There is no condemnation but being restored into right relationship with God demands a higher standard. We go forth into our future with a new-found resolve to live above the sin which the cross destroyed. The rules do apply to us.

Father, forgive me today for setting standards in my life that may be contrary to your standards. I am truly grateful for salvation, and I want to live a life that truly reflects the work you have done in me. You freed me from sin that I can go and sin no more. Even when temptations come, give me the power and grace to rise above them and always live according to the standards of your word in the shadow of the cross. In Christ's name, amen.

TWELFTH DAY OF LENT
TUESDAY
"THE LIGHT OF THE WORLD"

Reading: John 8:12-20

Jesus spoke to them again: "I am the light of the world. Anyone who follows me will never walk in the darkness but will have the light of life."

JOHN 8:12 (CSB)

EACH NIGHT OF THE GREAT FEAST of Sukkot, four giant lights were illuminated in the courtyard of the temple. Torches were also lit and carried by the masses as the musicians played and the people sang and rejoiced. The brightened temple mount in Jerusalem during the Feast of Tabernacles was transformed into a giant outdoor night of worship and praise. I can imagine looking from the hills surrounding the city and witnessing the glow of lights cutting through the darkness, providing a festive atmosphere for God's people to celebrate their freedom.

As He had done with the water ceremony, Jesus seized the moment to make the connection between Himself and what was happening around Him. "You see all this incredible light piercing through the darkness? That's me! I am the light, but not just a light for a courtyard party, I am the light of the world!"

To gain context for Jesus' incredible claim, we go back 1,400 years to the book of Exodus. During the 40 years of wilderness wandering, God led the vast nation of more than two million people by a pillar of fire at night to light the way forward. Whenever the nation stopped and camp was set, the fire never left, but rested inside the cloud of glory covering the tabernacle, God's dwelling place. What Jesus declared to the sea of people on this illuminated night in Jerusalem would have been understood fully by those in the courtyard. Jesus gave an invitation to follow Him, and by following, it would be just like following the pillar of fire which illuminated the wilderness. Jesus declared Himself to be the One who provides the way for all people to be led through the darkness covering the Earth.

On July 13, 1977, New York City, the largest city in the U.S., was hit by a blackout. The city's power grids failed and for more than eight hours in the thick of the night, darkness ruled, and chaos ensued. More than 1,000 stores were looted resulting in economic loss of more than $300 million. Police were assaulted by angry mobs and four people were murdered as darkness covered the city.

God responded to the darkness in creation by saying, "Let there be light." In doing so, our Creator established the truth that darkness, no matter how thick and powerful, cannot win when light is present. Jesus is that light and His invitation to a celebrating crowd in the temple courtyard on a fall evening was this: "if you follow me, darkness won't win. I will go before you exactly like the fire in the wilderness to illuminate your way. There may be chaos all around you, but just follow me. You will have the light of life, not as a possession to own, but a relationship to enjoy."

Jesus, however, is on a journey to the cross and while this message at the feast is loaded with celebration, hope, and encouragement, there will be challenges ahead to overcome. Even when such challenges rise, we can camp out around His abiding presence and follow Him on this journey with the confidence that darkness will not win. Light always prevails.

Father, as I look at the world, it is easy to see the darkness which appears to be winning the day. The anger, hatred, and violence characterizing the world are a result of those who refuse to walk in the light of your Son. People are blinded by the darkness and cannot see that through your Son, a way has been made to walk in light. I pray His light will penetrate the darkness of this world and those who are groping in darkness will see that Jesus, and Jesus alone, is the light of life. In Christ's name, amen.

———————————————

THIRTEENTH DAY OF LENT
WEDNESDAY
"THE MAN BORN BLIND"

Reading: John 9:1-41

"Neither this man nor his parents sinned," Jesus answered. "
This came about so that God's works might be displayed in him.

JOHN 9:3 (CSB)

IT'S YOUR FAULT! It's his fault! It's her fault! It's someone's fault! Someone must take the blame for this catastrophe. Blame shifting is what human beings do and it has been that way from the beginning of time. Anytime there is a tragedy or injustice, someone must assume responsibility and take the fall. If the economy is in the tank, each political side blames the other. When there is a natural disaster, sides are drawn and it's either God's fault or someone must have sinned to spawn the calamity.

Let's make it personal. When illness strikes or there is bankruptcy, divorce, addiction, trauma, anxiety, or depression invading our experience, we want to know the cause. If we can determine the cause, we can then assign responsibility and blame. That is what Jesus' disciples wanted to do when they encountered a man born blind. The Light of the World was present with them, yet they still looked for a cause. "Who sinned, this guy or his parents? He was born blind, and someone is responsible." The focus of the disciples is not on the person, or even God's purpose for the person. Their focus is on the cause. What's more, they are looking to the past, even to generational dynamics, to try and sort this out.

We are prone to do the same. Unhealthy and unbiblical teaching about generational curses keeps people anchored in the past and unable to move into their future. There is no doubt our past affects our present and sometimes we do need to go back and deal with the dynamics of our past to go forward. Circumstances, events, and decisions made in one generation affect another, but that is not Christ's focus with this man born blind. His focus was not on who sinned in the past and affected the present, it was on leveraging the present for the future. "This came about so that God's works might be displayed in him" (John 9:3).

Jesus doesn't look for cause, He looks for meaning and this is a radical shift for all who look at past events to make sense of present reality. Just as Jesus directs His focus to this man's future, we must also look for the meaning of our present while considering our future. We may not have a great explanation of our present circumstances, but it will come as we allow God to work and bring it to completion. Christ's death made no sense until the resurrection, and as Paul so brilliantly declared...

For I consider that the sufferings of this present time are not worthy to be compared with the glory which shall be revealed in us. (Romans 8:18 NKJ)

Life is really about what we make of it, and what God makes of it through us as we trust and follow Him. When I had my own personal self-destruction, I didn't need anyone to help me focus on the causes. Oh yes, my therapist helped unearth some things from my past which undoubtedly affected my choices, but as I stood broken, humbled, and shamed by where I ended up, I was determined not to stay mired in my present reality, no matter the circumstances that got me there. I stood before my Savior, submitted to His plan, and He eventually made something beautiful out of a junk yard.

God had a far greater purpose than what I could see. In essence, I was like the blind man in our story – unable to see. Yet as the Light shined into me, my eyes were opened to the truth that in Christ, all things find purpose and meaning. What does He want to do with your present circumstance? Let's stop looking for who to blame and look to the One we can trust to help us see His glory.

Father, I know there are things in my present anchored to my past. Today, open my eyes to see you don't want me to stay stuck in my current reality, but you indeed want to give me a hope and a future. Today I believe you alone can take something ugly and turn it into something beautiful, so I take the ugliness of my situation and place it in your hands to do a great work and reveal your glory in my life. In Christ's name, amen.

———————————————————

FOURTEENTH DAY OF LENT
THURSDAY
"THE GOOD SHEPHERD"

Reading: John 10:1-21

"I am the good shepherd. The good shepherd lays down his life
for the sheep."

JOHN 10:11 (CSB)

ONE OF THE FIRST PASSAGES OF SCRIPTURE I learned as a child was Psalm 23. "The Lord is my Shepherd…" I committed it to memory in the poetic style of the King James Version, and still love the way the Psalmist uses the metaphor of the shepherd to describe our LORD who leads, guides, protects, restores, and provides for His people, His sheep. As Jesus journeyed toward His destiny, He picked up this beautiful theme of shepherding and applied it to Himself. As He had done at the Feast of Tabernacles, He continues His declaration of bringing light and life to all who will come and follow. Yet, in this exchange with those still uncertain about His identity, Jesus differentiates:

The thief comes only to steal and kill and destroy. I came that
they may have life and have it abundantly.

I am the good shepherd... (John 10:10-11a ESV)

Jesus is saying, "If you follow me, you will have an abundant, overflowing cup of life, just as Psalm 23 promises. I am the source. I guide you here and call you to it. I am the good shepherd." The "thief" is almost always recognized as Satan whose sole purpose from the beginning of creation has been to keep us from the tree of life by deceit, plunder, murder, and destruction. But this reference would have spoken to the first hearers of other shepherds who were not good yet paraded as such.

At the time of Jesus, the people of Israel lived under the intense oppression of the Roman Empire and longed to be free from its tyranny and domination. Many individuals came along around the time of Christ who promised freedom but went about it the wrong way. One was Athronges, the Shepherd, who gathered a band of brothers, crowned himself king and over a two-year period murdered several garrisons of Roman soldiers before being squashed by the Empire. There was also an able-bodied slave of Herod named Simon who declared himself King of the Jews. He burned the royal palace at Jericho to the ground along with other royal residences in the country, taking the spoils in the process. Yet another freedom-promiser was Judas, the son of Ezekias, who plundered and robbed the royal palace at Sepphoris and became known for his brutal treatment of others.

One could say these pseudo-messiahs, kings, and shepherds came only to steal, kill and destroy. Jesus said, "I'm not like that. I am a good shepherd. I am not one who takes life, but one who gives life. I don't bring destruction. I build up lives, lifting the oppressed from their bondage and elevating them to a special place in God's Kingdom." Jesus models a different way of leading others as He is willing to lay down His own life for the sake of the sheep. When we choose to follow Jesus, this is the kind of shepherd we follow. We follow Him and then goodness and mercy follow us throughout life, granting us an eternal dwelling place in His house. Learn His voice, and hear Him, as our Lord said on the mountain. Then follow Him, the Good Shepherd, because in Him is abundant life.

Father, I long for the abundant life your Son came to bring and to see abundant life realized in others. I have seen theft, murder, and destruction wreak havoc over the world for too long. People are following shepherds who are only out for their own selfish gain but today, the truth of the Good Shepherd has captured my heart. I renew my commitment to follow His leading, trusting He will indeed lead me where I need to go. May the world see that He is indeed the Good Shepherd who lays down His life for His sheep. In Christ's name, amen.

FIFTEENTH DAY OF LENT
FRIDAY
"THE SEVENTY-TWO"

Reading: Luke 10:1-12

Now go; I am sending you out like lambs among wolves. Don't carry a money bag, traveling bag, or sandals...

LUKE 10:3-4a (CSB)

IN 2004, GWEN AND I left the shores of the United States for the first time. Our destination was Arusha, Tanzania, and our primary assignment was to introduce music to a privately funded school in the remote village of Magugu. We were well-stocked for the trip – plenty of changes of clothes, extra shoes, a couple of credit cards, adequate cash, and several bottles of insect repellant. Our base was a walled compound with cozy huts and internet access which was slow dial-up, but at least we could access email. We also had cell phones, but no carriers in those days had cheap, international plans. Calling home was short and expensive, but at least we could say 'hi' to our kids.

On the trip, I also taught at a Bible school and preached in local churches. It was missions work, but it was very safe other than the snake I saw which enabled me to unofficially break the world record in the 100. Overall, it was comfortable. The food was great, and our hosts were gracious. I would do it again in a heartbeat, knowing this time I could take a laptop and have Zoom along with unlimited text and talk. Missions work.

Jesus sending out the 72 is meant to show us that following Him and committing to His mission in the world requires two things: sacrifice and trust. Informing His followers they were being sent like lambs among wolves was more than a clever simile. Upon hearing this, they inherently knew among wolves, lambs did not survive. Lambs were defenseless with no capacity to self-protect against the stronger, more powerful animals lying in wait. For the 72 being sent this meant sacrifice and trust, with a willingness to die if necessary.

Even if we do not find ourselves in harm's way, an honest reading of the New Testament reveals that as followers of Jesus, we live as though we are dead. We are daily bearing our cross as living sacrifices, continually being formed into the image of the One who calls and sends us. We sacrifice and are willing to do whatever it takes. Missions work.

The next part is equally, if not more challenging. "Don't take anything for the journey." Surely this is hyperbole, right? I don't think so. Jesus wanted His sent ones to fully depend on and trust Him for everything including their food, clothing, and financial provision. "Don't take a carry-on, or even a fanny-pack. No extra shoes despite the rocky, thorny terrain.

Just go. Speak the Shalom of God over households. If they welcome it, great. If not, move on to the next place. I will take care of you."

I don't know if I have that kind of faith. I don't know if I have that kind of sacrificial mentality because I like certainty. I like knowing I have enough money, food, and clothing. I like my internet, smart phone, comfortable car, hot shower, and air conditioning. Yet every day, I am being sent as a sheep among wolves. Our culture is a devouring one looking for vengeance and retribution. It will cancel us in a heartbeat if we don't conform or agree with its evil ways. It seeks to devour the truth and sabotage the way of Jesus as being intolerant, bigoted, and oppressive.

In some ways, being in everyday culture in the West is far less secure than our walled Arusha compound in Tanzania. We must be willing to sacrifice, stand for truth, and continue to speak the Shalom of God, whether it is received or not. Ultimately, we trust Christ will abundantly supply all we need, sometimes coming from the least likely places. The Kingdom has indeed come near, and two of its greatest qualities are sacrifice and trust, especially among wolves. Missions work.

Father, forgive me for the times I have sought ease and comfort over sacrifice and trust. Keep my eyes focused on your mission and remind me that when culture is fighting and pushing against your way and your Kingdom, you will provide all I need. Remove fear from my heart, knowing that even among wolves, you are there to lead, guide, and protect your sheep. In Christ's name, amen.

SIXTEENTH DAY OF LENT
SATURDAY
"THE RIGHT QUESTION"

Reading: Luke 10:25-37

Which of these three...proved to be a neighbor...?
The one who showed mercy..."

LUKE 10:36-37 (CSB)

I GREW UP IN A GOOD NEIGHBORHOOD. It was neither fancy nor situated behind a coded gate. The homes were small and modest, with no garages but had decent sized yards to play in. Most of the families in the neighborhood had kids who all went to the same school and knew where each other lived. We rode bikes together across the neighborhood and it wasn't uncommon for 10-15 of my friends to gather in the mornings at my house for us walk to school together. It was a different world and a different time, but the memories are fond. As the years passed, however, the neighborhood changed. Recently, my day's travel provided a detour through the old neighborhood, and I was shocked to see houses falling into disrepair and the socio-economic factors taking a toll on what was once a vibrant community.

Pulling out from local neighborhoods, the "neighborhood" of our world has changed drastically in recent decades. In the West, there was once a collective consciousness of God, a mutual agreement He existed, and even if one did not confess Christianity, there was a moral code of sorts which held the fabric of the neighborhood together. Not so anymore. Religious pluralism, moral relativism, and self-identity rule the day. The neighborhood has changed.

The question asked of Jesus by the lawyer as a matter of self-justification is still being asked by us. "And who is my neighbor?" It was a trap question and Jesus knew it. We know it was a trap because the lawyer stood up. In the culture of Jesus' day, a true disciple sat at the feet of the teacher and listened. By standing up, the lawyer served notice on the room he had no intention of being a disciple of Jesus, and he only had one desire – to demonstrate what he knew rather than what he was willing to do. By asking "who is my neighbor," the lawyer revealed a heart set on choosing for himself whom to love and show mercy to. He wanted to survey the neighborhood and find those he deemed worthy.

Jesus, the master teacher, answered with a story which made a despised Samaritan the hero all because he was willing to be the neighbor. This is really the essence of what it means to love our neighbor – be the neighbor, even when the neighborhood is changing. The Good Samaritan strikes a decisive blow to all forms of social and ethnic prejudice, teaching us that true disciples of Jesus are those who extend love, mercy, compassion no matter what the cost or comfort level. This story also shows us having right doctrine and moral purity mean nothing if, when facing the brokenness of humanity, we refuse to act. The lawyer who refused discipleship had both, but as Jesus pointed out, it wasn't enough. Someone said, "It's not right to be right unless it rights a wrong." God is looking for disciples who will listen to their Rabbi, stay at His feet, and heed His call to action.

Even in the neighborhood of my youth there was brokenness underneath the veneer of community. We just didn't always see it. Now, thanks to technology and social media, the brokenness of our world lies constantly at our fingertips. The entire world has become our neighborhood. Let's not ask "who is my neighbor?" but rather, "how can I be the neighbor when the neighborhood is changing?"

Father, I recognize the rapid pace at which our world is changing. At times, when I see the brokenness of our world it becomes overwhelming. I want to help, but I don't know how. I ask today that you would lead me by your Spirit to one person I can be the neighbor to. Let it begin there. Show me one who needs your love, grace, mercy, and compassion. Pull me away from myself and my own selfishness to simply pour into someone else. In Christ's name, amen.

THIRD SUNDAY OF LENT

"THE NECESSARY THING"

Reading: Luke 10:38-42

...but one thing is necessary. Mary has made the right choice.

LUKE 10:42 (CSB)

THE JOURNEY TO THE CROSS is more than steps taken. It is lessons learned. It reveals to us the state of our own discipleship and what it really means to follow Jesus. The goal of being a disciple of Christ is not a mansion over the hilltop in the sweet by and by where we dance on streets of gold for eternity. It is knowing Him and becoming one with Him.

This little vignette in Luke's travel narrative pulls together many essentials of discipleship which command our attention. Historically, Martha has been criticized for busyness, and consuming her energies with being a good host as she vilifies her sister as one who is lazy and uncaring about the details of near-Eastern hospitality. Jesus uses this moment to underscore the importance of something we saw in yesterday's reading with the lawyer – posture. Luke tells us Martha...

...had a sister name Mary who also sat at the Lord's feet...
(Luke 10:39 CSB emphasis added)

The tiny word "also" indicates Martha and Mary shared the same posture of sitting at the Lord's feet, the posture of a disciple, one who has a listening ear and longs to be taught the ways of the Kingdom by the Savior Himself. Martha's problem is not her overall posture and willingness to sit at the Lord's feet. Like many of us, Martha was distracted and drawn away by her task list. She had things to do, important things which required her attention. She needed help and let everyone in the room, including Jesus know it. These distractions drew Martha away from what Jesus called "the necessary thing." Thayer's Greek Lexicon defines "necessary" as "sustenance for the journey." Jesus did not rebuke Martha. He simply reminded her good things can pull us away from the necessary thing which is to remain at His feet and hear His voice. The sustenance for Martha's journey would not come from continuing at a hectic pace, or even getting the help she desired from Mary. It would only come through practicing the necessary thing.

We live in a distracted world where life pulls us in multiple directions. We fill our calendars to the breaking point, scheduling ourselves into a frenzy. Most likely, the things we fill our lives with are good things – work, family, recreation, etc. All things God wants us to delight in. Our hearts may be in the posture of a disciple who takes time to sit and listen, but our actions say otherwise. The message of Jesus to Martha is clear. Don't neglect the necessary thing.

I am prone to this. As a husband, father, grandfather, pastor, teacher, church coach, and leader, I have a full plate. Sometimes I take on the martyr complex of Martha – "Nobody cares! Nobody is helping! God, please get some lazy people off their rear ends to jump in and help!" Perhaps this is an unhealthy need for recognition, and maybe it was Martha's underlying problem. Maybe it's yours. The solution? Our life of doing good things for Jesus cannot outweigh the necessary thing, the posture of simply being with Jesus.

Father, today I confess that I am a busy person living in a busy world. The distractions to my own discipleship are plentiful and even though my heart is to know you deeply and intimately, my actions at times say otherwise. I know many of the things I fill my life with are good things, but I do not want to sacrifice the best at the expense of the good. Allow my life to stay in a posture that reflects my desire to know you – to sit at your feet and listen. Being with you is the necessary thing. In Christ's name, amen.

SEVENTEENTH DAY OF LENT
MONDAY
"THE PERSISTENT FRIEND"

Reading: Luke 11:5-13

...yet because of his friend's shameless boldness, he will get up and give him as much as he needs.

LUKE 11:8b (CSB)

MY KIDS HAVE ALWAYS BEEN PERSISTENT, especially my youngest daughter, Charity. Gwen and I have long believed she could have been captain of a school debate team because once she is set on getting something, she refuses to quit until it becomes reality. Trying to be good parents, we don't acquiesce to everything – at least Gwen doesn't. After all, I am a dad, and it's my daughter. What can I say? Charity has the gift of "shameless persistence" and that is really the point of this parable Jesus uses to illustrate what we, as His disciples, need when it comes to our prayer life.

Earlier in Luke 11, the disciples asked Jesus to teach them to pray and Jesus responded, giving His closest followers what we refer to as The Lord's Prayer. To describe the disposition of heart required in prayer, Jesus told the story of a man needing food for unexpected guests who arrived at his home late at night. Having no food, the man seeks out a nearby friend, relentlessly knocks on the door and persistently asks until the friend opens the door and supplies the need. The man's shameless boldness is best described as "raw nerve," and I see it as the kind of faith we need in prayer as we go before the Lord to ask, seek, and knock.

We have such a limited view of faith at times, trying to muster up a pseudo-belief that is never tangible, but exists only in the invisible realm. While there is an element of faith requiring belief in the unseen, true faith also requires action. For Jesus, active faith is unyielding persistence and unrelenting determination which refuses to give up, no matter what. Seek relentlessly, ask shamelessly, knock persistently, and the door will be open to you. I have always been bothered by verse 10 in this parable.

> For everyone who asks receives, and the one who seeks finds,
> and to the one who knocks, the door will be opened.
> (Luke 11:10 CSB)

How many times have we asked and not received? Many. For me, it has caused me to question God and buy into a belief system which says He's unreliable, and unconcerned about my situation. Then I realize, in Christ's perspective, "everyone" is not everyone. Jesus is saying "everyone who has the disposition of the guy at the door – the persistent friend – who asks, receives."

Persistent faith is Jacob wrestling with God and saying, "I won't let you go until you bless me." It's Elijah at the top of Mt. Carmel soaking the altar three times with water and still expecting the fire to fall. It's Paul praying three times to gain a true understanding of sufficient grace. It's Moses at the Red Sea lifting his hands to the LORD when he was out of options. It's marching around Jericho for seven days in silence. It's staring down a wicked king who demands your worship, knowing a furnace has been kindled for you. It's an attitude that says, "I won't quit no matter what" and having the resolve to ask, seek, and knock. It's the kind of persistence that will make a teenage daughter stand up and leap with joy.

Father, today I ask for a new level of faith to rise in my spirit. Forgive me for the times I have given up in prayer and renew an attitude of shameless persistence in my life that refuses to give up. I bring all my situations before you today that seem hopeless and stand at the door, willing to ask, seek, and knock until the door is opened. I recognize my own limitations and invite your Holy Spirit to stand with me, instilling boldness in my life. In Christ's name, amen.

EIGHTEENTH DAY OF LENT
TUESDAY
"THE HEALTHY EYE"

Reading: Luke 11:14-36

Your eye is the lamp of the body. When your eye is healthy,
your whole body is also full of light...

LUKE 11:34 (CSB)

VISION PROBLEMS RUN IN MY FAMILY. My grand-mother passed them on to my dad, he passed them on to my sister and me, and two of my four biological children have inherited the stellar Jennings vision. When my youngest son, Chandler, was about three years old he started walking into walls and furniture. We thought he was just clumsy. Turns out, he couldn't see. Each year when I visit the eye doctor, it's the same routine – let's see how we can tweak the lenses enough to keep the vision clear. It's a never-ending cycle, but sight is important. Cloudy, blurry vision is frustrating and affects everything.

Jesus knew this from a practical standpoint. He seized a moment when many were on the fence about following Him to emphasize the importance of having clear, focused, single vision. It was a discipleship mandate to stop looking for the wrong things and focus solely on things that matter. Jesus performed tangible miracles right in front of crowds – healings, exorcisms, even resurrections from the dead, yet the people continued to ask for a sign. Jesus didn't budge. "You're either with me or against me. You're either following or you're not. The double vision issue you have comes from your own desires, and you want what is right in your own eye. You want the blessings of following me, yet you are double-minded and unstable. That's not how the Kingdom works."

> Blessed are those who hear the word of God and keep it.
> (Luke 11:28 CSB)

We need the singleness of heart which only comes from having clear eyes and this is only possible as we forsake our ways for His ways. If we are paying attention, we see a pattern emerging in Jesus' call to discipleship which began in Caesarea Philippi, continued to the Transfiguration and the feast at Jerusalem. Choose Him. Hear Him. Follow Him.

Jesus made it clear to the crowd in this poignant moment – "if you want a sign, look at Jonah and his preaching at Nineveh where an entire generation repented and was saved. One greater than Jonah is here. You want wisdom? People came. The Queen of Sheba came seeking the wisdom of Solomon and one greater than Solomon is here."

Christ wants to make us a light for the nations, but we

must see clearly with singleness of vision, loving Him with heart, soul, mind, strength, and loving neighbor as ourselves. When I see life through this eye, I no longer see double, run into walls, or try to find a way to have my cake and eat it too. Seeing through a clear, single lens allows me to see what my Lord requires, for my eyes are fixed on Him. I allow His life to become my life, and as Jesus said, my whole body becomes full of light. Then and only then can the world see Him through me. No fences. No signs. No double vision. Only Jesus.

When my dark night of the soul came to its peak in 2018, this was the life I knew I had to find and the years since have brought the importance of clarity and singleness of heart to the forefront in my own life. I know this works and as a result, the following poetic expression from Psalm 27 has become my life verse. May it come alive in you as well.

One thing I ask from the LORD, this only do I seek; that I may dwell in the house of the Lord all the days of my life, to gaze on the beauty of the LORD and to seek him in his temple.
(Psalm 27:4 NIV)

Father, I ask today that you reveal the blind spots in my life. Show me why my vision is blurry and cloudy. Search my heart and open the areas where I have become double-minded and unstable. Bring it all to the surface so I can lay it before you in humble repentance. Forgive me for seeking things other than you to fill the deep longings of my life. I renew my commitment to fix my eyes upon you as the author and finisher of my faith. Singleness of heart is what I seek. In Christ's name, amen.

NINETEENTH DAY OF LENT
WEDNESDAY
"THE WINTRY HEART"

Reading: John 10:22-42

The Festival of Dedication took place in Jerusalem, and it was winter.

JOHN 10:22 (CSB)

WINTER IS MY FAVORITE SEASON. Now, depending on what winter is like where you live, this may cause you to tilt your head in wonder. Bear in mind my home is in the Sonoran Desert of Arizona where the summers are brutally hot, and winter offers a time of respite from the blistering heat. Traditionally, winter is associated with cold, frigid temperatures, snow, ice, and dormancy. New things don't spring to life in winter as the ground becomes hard and frozen, creating a barrier that allows no seed in and no growth out.

John makes the point to us in this passage that the Festival of Dedication happened in winter, thus creating the context for this powerful moment in the journey to the cross. Though not a biblical feast, the Festival of Dedication was the celebration of a miraculous moment in Israel's history which took place two centuries before Christ. In 167 BCE, Antiochus Epiphanes, a Seleucid king and anti-christ figure, desecrated the temple of God and turned it into a pagan shrine. Judas Maccabeus, also known as Judas the Hammer, led a revolt, defeated Antiochus, and regained control of the temple. When the temple was rededicated to the LORD, they only had enough oil to light the menorah for one day. Miraculously, the oil lasted eight days providing the necessary lighting in the Holy Place. Eventually, this festival became known as the Festival of Lights, and we know it today as Hanukkah.

Jerusalem is cold in the winter, and it is possible on this occasion the Holy City received snowfall as the lights of the festival burned brightly in the homes of the residents. The cold without was a microcosm of the cold within the hearts of many as they continued their quest to trap Jesus. Asking our LORD to "tell us plainly" and end the suspense of whether He was the Messiah was not the inquiry of a seeking heart, but rather an inquisition from a cold, stony, frozen heart. Their minds were already made up. Nothing Jesus could say would make a difference. The winter ground was hard and frozen. No seed could go in and no fruit could come out.

> ...the works I do in my Father's name testify about me. But you don't believe because you are not of my sheep.
> (John 10:25b-26 CSB)

Taking up stones to get rid of Jesus was more than a physical act by the crowd. It was a spiritual act flowing from the hardened hearts of those who refused to believe.

What is the condition of your heart? Is it open and receptive or cold and frozen? To see Jesus is to see God and He is the perfect revelation of the Father. True disciples hear His words, recognizing they are spirit and life. Disciples follow the Good Shepherd and journey with the One who leads beside still waters and restores the soul. Disciples don't base their lives on what they want, but their desire is for the One who has revealed Himself as being one with the Father in essence, purpose, and action. Moreover, disciples burn the light brightly, refusing to allow the wintry pull of a cold and frozen heart to identify their lives.

Father, today I reflect on the season of my heart. I admit at times my discipleship journey becomes challenging and I must guard against the wintry thrust that pushes against the vitality and growth you desire for me. I truly want my heart to receive what you want to give, and bear fruit that glorifies you. Break up the frozen ground of my life. Thaw out the areas of cold indifference and prepare my heart for a new season of life and growth. In Christ's name, amen.

TWENTIETH DAY OF LENT
THURSDAY
"THE NARROW DOOR"

Reading: Luke 13:22-30

Make every effort to enter through the narrow door, because I tell you, many will try to enter and won't be able.

LUKE 13:24 (CSB)

BOUNDARIES ARE GOOD. That's what I told our kids, anyway. Most of the time they weren't thrilled with the boundaries we set for them, but of course, parents know best. Boundaries are really for one purpose — to teach us how to manage our freedom, and this has been God's perspective from the beginning of time.

In the Garden of Eden, the forbidden tree was not perched atop an inaccessible mountain, but right smack in the middle, open and accessible. The irony is the entire garden was at humanity's disposal. "Freely eat from any tree," God said, "but there is a boundary. You see that tree in the middle of the garden? Off limits." To our forebears, it must have felt restricting, much like children feel when parents limit screen time or set a curfew. But boundaries are good. The enemy knew this and exploited it. Humanity took the bait, and the results were disastrous. By eating from the forbidden tree, humanity abandoned a narrow way for a broad way and rather than enjoying full-on freedom with boundaries, they were now on the outside of real freedom looking in. They now lived in a world of self-made freedom, but when it came to God's best, His perfection, the door was shut, all because they abandoned a "restrictive way" for their own way.

The way of Jesus is narrow and if we are honest, it can seem restricting. The narrow way, however, is the best way and ultimately, there is an entire garden of goodness from which we may freely eat. Juxtapose that with the way of hardship and suffering accompanying the narrow way of Christ. At times it may feel like walking through a narrow, lonely, and desolate canyon, but it is an opening to a new reality of abundant living. Those who have chosen their own door find themselves, like Adam and Eve, on the outside looking in, weeping, and gnashing their teeth with regret, knowing they are reaping the consequences of their own decisions.

A good friend of mine once said, "straight doesn't seem exciting unless you've lived a crooked path." Pause and consider that statement. At first glance, the narrow way of Jesus feels restrictive, but at the end of Jesus' parable in today's reading, those who choose not to enter are the ones filled with distress and regret because they have recognized the futility of living outside the boundaries. For those now outside, freedom became futile. The crooked path proved incapable of lasting satisfaction as the strait, narrow way brimmed with adventure, excitement, and true freedom.

Our task as those who have entered the narrow door to walk the strait way is to manage our freedom, and never find ourselves on the opposite side of the door. Many have tried to pigeon-hole this parable into a reflection on eternal judgment, and that may well be the case. All scripture, however, is given to us for instruction in righteousness and as our journey to the cross picks up steam, the stakes become even higher. Don't seek the easy way. It's crooked and will ultimately fail to satisfy. Seek the boundary of the narrow door and find freedom.

Father, I recognize the boundaries you have set are good. Everything in me fights against these boundaries but I know you see everything with the end in mind, and your plans for me are to give a hope and a future. Knowing this, I place my life today in your hands. Give me the grace to walk your way when everything else says for me to do my own thing and make myself happy. I don't want to ever be on the outside of your blessing no matter how challenging it may be to enter the narrow door. Your grace is sufficient, and I lean in. In Christ's name, amen.

TWENTY-FIRST DAY OF LENT
FRIDAY
"THE COST"

Reading: Luke 14:25-35

For which of you, wanting to build a tower, doesn't first sit down
and calculate the cost to see if he has enough to
complete it?

LUKE 14:28 (CSB)

IMPULSE BUYING is never a good idea. The impulse area at the grocery store is loaded with things to eat or read that seem good in the moment but are unhealthy for consumption. Do we really need that extra pack of M&M's or this week's edition of *The Enquirer*? Probably not and retailers know this. Rash decisions make money. Impulse buying, however, is not limited to the area by the checkout stand. Consumers make rash decisions about major appliances, clothing, cars, and even homes. The economic landscape is littered with defaults, foreclosures, and bankruptcies that in many cases are a result of impulsive financial decisions and not counting the cost. This short teaching on the road to Jerusalem undoubtedly shocked Jesus' traveling companions as He reminded them of the great cost of discipleship that is both challenging and high.

God wants to build our lives by continuous growth and transformation. If we allow Him to, this construction project will last a lifetime and He will ultimately bring it to completion. He doesn't want us to stand as an unfinished building project which falls into disrepair and could collapse at any moment. He wants to prepare us for battles where it may seem there are more against us than with us. In those moments, we dig deep, lean in, take our focus off the battle itself and place our confidence in the God of the battle. In this regard, the cost is worth it.

The most shocking element of this powerful exhortation on counting the cost is the call to hate our families as a prerequisite for discipleship. I struggle with this. My family is everything to me and I will do anything and everything to guarantee their safety and security. In a culture with a base foundation of honoring father and mother, it is a wonder Jesus would appear to violate the fifth commandment by making such an outrageous claim. We can't anesthetize "hate" as simply being the opposite of "love," so how do we reconcile the cost of discipleship with the high value God places on honoring our families? The answer may lie in the way the rabbis of Israel taught the following verse.

Every one of you shall revere his mother and his father, and you shall keep my sabbaths; I am the Lord your God.
(Leviticus 19:3 ESV)

The rabbis taught if parents went against the ways of God, disregarding and discouraging those ways, don't listen to them. As part of our mandate to count the cost of discipleship we may find that people close to us, even our families, show disregard for us following the way of Jesus. They may go as far as to say, "don't waste your time following a religion or those crazy, antiquated, and irrelevant teachings." Going back to Jesus' statement, we hate this alternative. We then demonstrate a willingness to count this very high cost and follow the way of Jesus no matter what.

I can love my family, but if they try to deter me from pursuing eternal life by following the way of Jesus, I must be willing to dishonor and hate their call to go the opposite way. The stakes are high. The cost is great, but this is part of the cross we are called to bear. We follow Him no matter the cost.

Father, as the journey to the cross continues and we walk with you on the road to Jerusalem, we feel the intensity ramping up. The discipleship challenge is real, and we hear your voice calling us higher. Being a disciple is not for the faint of heart, and we must choose to allow you to build our lives on your foundation and not on the whims of our own impulses. When those close to us choose not to walk your way and even criticize us for following you, allow us to stand firm knowing your way is better. In Christ's name, amen.

TWENTY-SECOND DAY OF LENT
SATURDAY
"THE LOST"

Reading: Luke 15:1-10

I tell you, in the same way, there will be more joy in heaven
over one sinner who repents than over ninety-nine righteous
people who don't need repentance.

LUKE 15:7 (CSB)

I CAN'T FIND MY PHONE! I can't find my wallet! I can't find my keys! I once read an article stating in the span of our lifetime, we will spend more than six months looking for lost things. I can say with confidence I have already used up my six months, and then some. The parallel between our relentless search for lost things and Jesus' parables of things lost is remarkably accurate. We will leave no cushion, mattress, or car seat unturned to retrieve things important to us. We will grab flashlights (or use our phone if it's not lost), ask for help, and do whatever is necessary to recover what was lost.

What makes this familiar story interesting is the audience to whom Jesus spoke. Tax collectors and sinners joined the religious crowd to create a moment for Jesus to teach about one of the principal aspects of the Kingdom. He spells out with incredible detail in these relatable stories what is important to God. In the first parable, we encounter a shepherd who has 100 sheep, loses one, and makes a calculated decision that retrieving the one lost sheep matters more than staying with the 99. The lesson? No one is expendable. Everyone matters. Then, in the second parable, we encounter a woman who loses 10% of her coin collection and flips the house upside down to locate it. For the shepherd and the woman of the house, the lost matter more than the found.

As the religious leaders squirmed, the tax collectors and sinners in the room saw a flicker of hope. "Maybe there is hope for us! Maybe we can still be part of the flock, part of the collection." As always with Jesus' teaching, there is an interesting dichotomy at play. There is a dual emphasis on the one seeking the lost and the one who is lost, and subsequently repents. Both are important. There are times on the journey when we are lost, and God relentlessly seeks us out. Other times we stray away, become lost, and need to repent.

One could draw the conclusion from these parables that it is all about God seeking after us and it is His choice who will be included in the search and rescue operation. To stop there, however, is to stop short of human responsibility. The key phrase from our key verse is "in the same way." One sinner who chooses to repent starts a party in heaven "in the same way" as one who is sought out, found, and rescued. Both can happen. Both are costly and valuable because they were lost and now, they are found.

Make no mistake, the lost matter to God more than the found and the times we have strayed from the flock or fallen between the cushions, we can be confident our Good Shepherd will seek us out. Our incredible Master will leave nothing unturned, thereby, reflecting His deep love for us. Then there are those seasons when, on our own, we need to do an about-face, the proverbial 180 of repentance. We decide once and for all that our current path is unsustainable and in need of the safety and security only a flock or a coin collection can provide, so we head for home. Either way, lost people matter deeply to God and heaven is waiting to erupt when we are finally counted among the found.

Father, today I ask that you rekindle my passion for the lost. I have family and friends who have strayed and need rescuing. I have other family and friends who know where safety and security are but need to make the decision to come back. Today, I pray for both, knowing they all matter to you. Good Shepherd, go after the lost sheep and the lost coin. Also, turn rebellious hearts toward you. In Christ's name, amen.

FOURTH SUNDAY OF LENT

"THE FATHER"

Reading: Luke 15:11-31

Because this son of mine was dead and is alive again; he was lost and is found!

LUKE 15:24 (CSB)

I HAVE BEEN FORTUNATE as a parent. Not only do I have great kids, but I have also been blessed to never have a kid go rogue. Oh, they did some crazy things, and I am sure as with all parents there are things we have been left in the dark about, but nothing rose to the level of what happened with the one we call the prodigal son. Here, Jesus tells of a young man who asked for and received his share of the family estate, spent every dime, and found himself feeding pigs just to survive. One day he woke up, came to his senses, and realized his father's hired servants were faring better so he started the journey home.

I have read, preached, and reflected on this story many times. As much as I love how the father welcomes his son home, lavishes him with love, and throws a big feast to celebrate the return, there is one aspect of this parable that has always troubled me. Unlike the shepherd who lost one sheep and the woman who lost one coin, the father does not go after his son. If one of my children went rogue, I would have scoured the countryside, inquired of friends, sent out advance scout teams, hired private investigators, and left no stone unturned to find them. If we carefully read what Jesus said to the diverse crowd, we will see the father did indeed go after his son.

Oh yes, the father ran to the prodigal, but not until he saw him within distance of the house. Remember, this man had two sons and it was the older brother whom the father went after because whether the prodigal's sibling knew it or not, he too was lost. He was lost in his own world of self-righteousness, piety, and pride. "I wasn't the one who left," the older brother cried. "I stayed. I served in the house, dad, and you never so much as killed a goat so I could party with my friends, let alone a choice cow. Your other son wasted your estate and slept with hookers. I have done everything right and you do this for him?" By refusing to go into the feast, the older brother demonstrated he was equally lost as the prodigal, separated from true relationship with the father. This is the moment we see the father go after his lost older son.

> ...so the father came out and pleaded with him.
> (Luke 15:28 CSB)

The father left where he was to find his lost son. As we saw yesterday, there are times the father relentlessly pursues us because of his great love. Other times, as with the young prodigal, He allows us to reap the consequences of our own choices until we come to our senses and return home. Then there is also a third possibility for us. We can become like the older brother, not realizing despite all we do right, we can become equally lost and estranged from our Heavenly Father.

Jesus does not resolve the story but leaves the listeners hanging. We don't know if the older brother had a change of heart and eventually went to the party, but at its core, the parable is about seeing the father's love for both of his lost sons. Whether we are relentlessly pursued and carried, we have our own "aha" moment, or develop elder brother syndrome, the loving Father longs for relationships with all his children. That is a magnificent picture of a God whose love is perfect and unending.

Father, continue to reveal the ways of my heart. Open my eyes to see clearly where I stand. If I have gone rogue and become blinded by my own destructive ways, give me the grace to come to my senses and return to you. If I have stayed with you and become blinded by my own self-righteousness and pious pride, give me the grace to repent and love my brothers and sisters the way you love. In Christ's name, amen.

TWENTY-THIRD DAY OF LENT
MONDAY
"THE TEST"

Reading: Luke 16:1-13

And I say to you, make friends for yourselves from the wealth of unrighteousness, so that when it fails, they will take you into the eternal dwellings.

LUKE 16:9 (LSB)

THE PHARISEES, tax collectors, and sinners have dispersed, and Jesus is once again alone with the 12. He continues to equip the men who will eventually change the world with what they need to follow their Rabbi and live the ways of the Kingdom. In this influential story, Jesus deals a fatal blow to two misconceptions. First, the idea God only wants to fill our lives with wealth and material possessions. This is an inherent danger within the prosperity gospel. The second idea dispelled is if one has wealth and possessions, it is a bad thing. This plays into a judgmental, poverty-driven mindset equally as dangerous as the prosperity gospel. Rich versus poor is not the point here. What is done with wealth and possessions becomes the central focus of this parable as it connects discipleship with stewardship.

Scripture is clear God has a heart for the poor and needy, but in the same vein, the wealthy 1% are never accused of being evil. Money in and of itself is not evil, but for the disciple of Christ, it is a means by which we demonstrate faithfulness to God. Proper handling of wealth and possessions can either honor God or make war against God and the choice is ours. Jesus makes it known that wealth and possessions are temporal and will eventually crumble along with all the ways and kingdoms of the world, yet they are things we deal with daily which can be used to "make friends" and strengthen relationship with both God and humanity. There is, perhaps, no greater test of our discipleship than how we handle material things. If we can't handle minimum wage and steward it properly, there is no chance we can handle being a millionaire.

The shrewd manager in Jesus' story is praised by the owner for doing all he could do with what was entrusted to him and that is precisely what Jesus expects of His disciples. Ultimately, the way we handle money and possessions reveals the level of our trust in God from the lowest wage earners to the 1%.

My wife and I were recently invited to spend a weekend with an incredible couple at their beautiful 5,600 square foot home with breathtaking views of God's wonderful creation. Here was an entrepreneurial couple in their 70s who have been successful in business, but more successful in embodying the principles of Godly stewardship. Over dinner, they shared stories of doing missions for 21 years in Central America among the poor and needy, sacrificially giving of time and resources to bring the good news to those who needed to hear. When they came off the field, they had nothing – no house, no money, no jobs. But over the years, the couple have built businesses and stewarded them in such a way they continue to sow back into Kingdom work at unprecedented levels. They get it. Wealth and possessions are not evil, but rather, a true mark of discipleship.

The challenge for us is to take what God gives us, no matter how great or small, and manage it well. Enjoy the fruit of labor but use it to bless others as shrewd managers making friends on the way to eternal dwellings.

Father, today I lay all my wealth and possessions before you whether great or small. I recognize these are gifts from you for me to steward and I commit myself this day to stewarding what you have provided. Forgive me for the times I have been a poor manager of what you have provided. I resolve this day to start fresh. I want the way I handle wealth and possessions to bring glory to your name and I choose to trust you in all things both great and small. In Christ's name, amen.

TWENTY-FOURTH DAY OF LENT
TUESDAY
"THE RESURRECTION OF LAZARUS"

Reading: John 11:1-44

Then Jesus, deeply moved again, came to the tomb...

JOHN 11:38a (CSB)

WE ARE EMOTIONAL BEINGS. God wired us to feel, and to deny our emotions or stuff them in the deep recesses of our soul is to be less than human. Throughout scripture we see a God who laughs, weeps, rejoices, experiences frustration, and becomes sorrowful. Jesus, being fully God and fully human, shows us the very nature of a God who feels deeply and is greatly touched by our own feelings, especially in our times of adversity.

Bethany is a mere two miles from Jerusalem on the eastern slope of the Mt. of Olives, and as Jesus arrives in the tiny village, His journey to the cross nears its climax. The death of His friend Lazarus, much to the angst of the disciples, draws Jesus near the place where His purpose would be fulfilled and the events which transpire in Bethany will set the wheels in full motion for God's redemptive plan to be completed. Jesus uses the tragic death of His friend to signal His complete control over death, but He also uses this moment to demonstrate the importance of confronting the full force of our emotions when faced with challenging situations.

Much of the emotional focus comes from the moment when Jesus wept. We love to see and feel this display of emotion as it connects Jesus to the sorrow of Mary, Martha, and the residents of Bethany. If we keep our focus solely on the God who weeps, we walk away with a powerful view of a God who is touched by our grief and sorrow, but this is not the only emotional connection we see with Jesus. While many in the crowd recognized the sincerity of Jesus' tears, the cynics in the throng said, "He healed the blind. Why couldn't He have prevented Lazarus from dying?"

At this, Jesus was "deeply moved," and approached the tomb where the dead man lay. The English translation does not do justice to the emotion on display in this moment. The word for "deeply moved" was used in classical Greek to describe the snorting of war horses before going into battle. It's a word of violent anger and as Jesus stands before the tomb of Lazarus, He is ready to go to battle against death and the grave. Satan may have temporary control, but that is about to end, and Jesus has no problem displaying what is happening in His soul. He has had enough, and He knows Satan's days are numbered. Jesus is tired of the grip death has held over humanity and knows the resurrection of Lazarus is the first nail in the devil's coffin. In just a few days, Jesus Himself will drive the final nail with His own death, burial, and resurrection.

The battle line is drawn in Bethany and our Lord is deeply moved like a war horse ready to charge forward. We should be grateful Jesus did not stuff or ignore His emotion. He is in touch with Himself as well as those around Him. He stands fearless before death and puts everything He feels inside on full display. The One who is the Resurrection and the Life is fully prepared to deal a blow to the one who has held humanity captive for too long.

Father, we are grateful you are a God who feels. You are touched by the pain, grief, and sorrow we experience in our broken world. We are grateful you went to battle on our behalf to fight and conquer death as the Resurrection and the Life and we look forward to the day when every tear will be wiped away and every wrong is made right. Because of you, we do not fear death, for it has been defeated and we anticipate the final resurrection in which we will all participate. In Christ's name, amen.

TWENTY-FIFTH DAY OF LENT
WEDNESDAY
"THE PLOT TO KILL JESUS"

Reading: John 11:45-57

...it is to your advantage that one man should die for the people rather than the whole nation perish

JOHN 11:50 (CSB)

FOR THE RELIGIOUS LEADERS seeking to get rid of Jesus, the resurrection of Lazarus was the tipping point. Right before their eyes stood an undeniable miracle and now, more than ever, people are flocking to the Rabbi from Galilee proclaiming Him as their Messiah. The reaction of Israel's religious leaders discloses to us that sometimes even miracles cannot change a hardened heart or a made-up mind.

For decades, the corrupt priesthood of Israel maintained a delicate political balance to secure the peace and safety of the nation which, at this point, was nothing more than a Roman-occupied territory. At the helm of this crooked group was one Joseph Caiaphas, a Sadducee appointed by Rome to function as the High Priest. Caiaphas succeeded his father-in-law, Annas, and was able to hold his seat of power for an unprecedented 18 years, the longest tenure of any High Priest in the first century. The irony of this arrangement with Rome cannot be lost. Here is a man who, according to Jewish law, was to stand as the mediator between Yahweh and His people, yet his real standing was as a political power broker caring for nothing but his own self-interests. The saying, "those who have power are afraid to lose it" certainly fit Caiaphas to the letter.

As the other members of the council fretted over losing their temple and nation, Caiaphas, whose words held great sway, told the Sanhedrin they had no idea what they were talking about. With great confidence, Caiaphas unveiled a carefully crafted plot from his politically and spiritually hardened heart which, unknown to him, aligned perfectly with the redemptive purpose of God. In truth, Joseph Caiaphas was the one who had no idea what he was talking about. His declaration that it was better to kill one for the sake of many was a prophetic pronouncement of what God was doing on Earth. In just a short time, Jesus would indeed die not only on behalf of the nation, but His death would also serve to bring all the lost children of God scattered throughout the Earth to rest under the banner of Yahweh's love and salvation. The council agreed with Caiaphas' assertion, and we read:

...from that day on, they plotted to kill him. (John 11:53)

When the plot was hatched, Jesus withdrew to a remote place with His disciples, but this was not a retreat in fear of

Caiaphas and his evil cohorts. The withdrawal was a sign to His followers that no person, group of persons, political entity, or empire would have the power to take His life. In accordance with God's plan and Christ's own volition, He would willingly lay down His life for all humanity when it was Yahweh's appointed time. Throughout the gospels Jesus declared "my hour has not yet come" and God alone holds times and seasons in His own authority. This serves as a wonderful reminder to us that God is always working things, no matter how challenging, to fulfill His purpose in our life. The intensity for Jesus will continue to climb as the journey to the cross progresses, and our own journeys may often become pressure packed. Let us always remember our journey is squarely under the control of a Redeemer who willingly laid down His life according to God's eternal purpose and sovereignly watches over us.

Father, there are days when I feel the pressure intensifying in my life. There are times and seasons when it seems like there is no purpose and the enemy is having his way. In these moments, may I recognize there is no evil that can supersede your plan and purpose for my life; and may I be reminded all things are indeed working together for my good because I am called according to your purpose. Release the pressure I feel to control outcomes and allow me to rest in the one who did not have His life taken, but willingly gave His life on my behalf. In Christ's name, amen.

TWENTY-SIXTH DAY OF LENT
THURSDAY
"THE OTHER NINE"

Reading: Luke 17:11-19

Jesus asked, "Didn't I heal ten men?
Where are the other nine?"

LUKE 17:17 (NLT)

EVERY DAY IS A GIFT. Each time the Earth makes its journey around the sun, and we behold the first glimpse of daylight, it reminds us God alone is the Creator and Sustainer of all things. Each day opens a fresh supply of mercies from a faithful and unchanging God in whom we live, move, and have our being. The dawning of a new day invites us to reflect deeply upon the One we serve and to live out the gift of our day in the strength of gratitude. Gratitude is a deep feeling of appreciation and flows from a life which truly recognizes what it has been given. What we have received from the LORD is unearned and undeserved, yet when we allow the depth of these gifts of grace to penetrate our heart, it will stimulate gratitude. We like to use the phrase "unmerited favor," to describe gifts of grace, and this is exactly what the 10 leprous men received when they were cleansed by Jesus from their ravaging disease.

Ten men discovered this unmerited gift of healing, but only one turned back to express gratitude to Jesus. By the way...he was a Samaritan. The gratitude from this former leper did not just happen. His first action after receiving his healing explains why, perhaps, the other nine failed to release any expression of thanksgiving. We are told the one who returned...

...with a loud voice gave glory to God. (Luke 17:15 CSB)

It was this release of exuberant praise and recognition of the One who gave the gift of healing that led to the expression of gratitude. The man knew he had been given an undeserved gift. He did nothing to earn or produce it. He simply responded in faith to Jesus' words and the healing came. Recognizing this gift, the man turned the posture of his heart toward God in worship. From that place of worship and giving glory to God, gratitude was released. The other nine undoubtedly felt the impact of the miracle, but because they failed to give glory to God first and foremost, gratitude had no base from which to be released. Praise releases gratitude.

When we ponder the gifts we have received from the LORD – a new day, family, employment, resources, or simply the breath in our lungs – let us recall this:

For everything comes from him and exists by his power and is
intended for his glory. All glory to him forever! Amen.
(Romans 11:36 NLT)

A willingness to give glory to God orients our heart in the
right direction. As we go on with our day, walking our journey, may we never cease to cry out with a loud voice, giving
glory to God. From that place of worship, may we always express gratitude for the gifts we have been freely and undeservedly given – most notably, our salvation. The leprosy of our
life, the stain of sin and stench of death, has been removed.
We are no longer societal outcasts, strangers, and foreigners
forced to live outside the camp in shame and disgrace. We
are now His sons and daughters who have received the gift of
salvation. We are now part of His family, and may we be like
the man who turned around after receiving his miracle. With a
loud voice, give glory to God and show gratitude.

*Father, I am grateful for the many gifts of grace you have
given me. They are too numerous to mention, but as I
ponder these gifts, may your unending goodness fill my
heart with gratitude. With a full heart, I praise you and
glorify you for the gifts received. With a loud voice I worship
you and pray that the orientation of my heart toward you will
allow me to live each day with gratitude. Thank you, Lord,
for all of your blessings, and especially for our salvation!
In Christ's name, amen.*

TWENTY-SEVENTH DAY OF LENT
FRIDAY
"THE RICH YOUNG MAN"

Reading: mark 10:17-22

Good teacher, what must I do...

MARK 10:17 (CSB)

HUMANS ARE DOERS. We do things with anticipation of results. We do our work with the anticipation of a paycheck. We do our housework with the anticipation of a clean dwelling place. Students do homework with the anticipation of a grade (and, of course, to avoid the wrath of parents). We do good things with the anticipation of earning God's favor. This is where it starts to break down.

For the first time in Jesus' ministry, He is asked a question not even His disciples were bold enough to ask. "What do I need to do in order to inherit eternal life?" The wealthy young man who asked this question was, like all of us, a doer. He had obviously done well for himself, checking all the boxes along the way. Saving regularly, check. Investing wisely, check. Debt avoidance, check. Business savvy, check. He had done all the right things to achieve worldly success and because he gained the anticipated results, now it was time to settle his eternal destiny with God. "What must I do to inherit eternal life? Jesus, show me the box so I can check it." Jesus knew what the young man was after and played along, but there is a twist He brings to the conversation, revealing a powerful truth about eternal life and the Kingdom: The inner life is more important than the outer life. One's state of being carries more weight than their state of doing.

The young man was quick to check the boxes of keeping what is written in the Torah. Don't murder, check. Don't commit adultery, check. Don't steal, check. Don't defraud your neighbor, check. Honor your parents, check. "Looks good, Jesus! I'm in! Ticket to heaven has been punched. Eternal life is secured." Jesus knew, however, that getting the externals right matter little if the interior life is disordered. A well-ordered life of doing cannot substitute for a disordered life of being. Doing all the right things is necessary, but ultimately incomplete if the interior life is not settled and oriented toward God. The young man's face told all when Jesus gave the directive to liquidate his assets and give the proceeds to the poor.

> At this, the man's face fell. He went away sad, because he
> had great wealth.
> (Mark 10:22 NIV)

In truth, this young man did not have his possessions. His possessions had him. His interior life was set on acquiring and keeping all he had done so much to obtain. As a result, despite all the right things he was doing to try and earn eternal life, he was losing his soul. In this moment, Jesus revealed the essence of what following Him is all about. He wants our heart. He desires an interior life whose affections are turned toward and ordered by Him. Love God with all your heart, soul, mind, and strength – and love your neighbor. Both work together. The young man may have gotten the last part right with all his good doings, but if not coupled with a heart turned to God, the life of doing is incomplete and incapable of receiving the eternal life God longs to give. For disciples of Christ, doing always flows from being.

Father, I know my life is naturally turned toward doing things to try and earn your favor. Turn my heart toward you first and foremost. Allow me to truly seek first your Kingdom and righteousness, trusting fully that all good things will be added unto me. Knowing you must be the priority of my life and loving you must be my primary affection. I cannot truly love my neighbor without loving you first, and at the same time, loving my neighbor reflects my love for you. Change my affections this day. In Christ's name, amen.

TWENTY-EIGHTH DAY OF LENT
SATURDAY
INTERLUDE -THE THIRD PREDICTION OF JESUS' DEATH

They were on the road, going up to Jerusalem, and Jesus was walking ahead of them. The disciples were astonished, but those who followed him were afraid. Taking the Twelve aside again, he began to tell them the things that would happen to him. "See, we are going up to Jerusalem. The Son of Man will be handed over to the chief priests and the scribes, and they will condemn him to death. Then they will hand him over to the Gentiles, and they will mock him, spit on him, flog him, and kill him, and he will rise after three days."

MARK 10:32-34 (CSB)

WITH THE PLOT TO KILL HIM in full swing, Jesus stood undeterred from His mission and purpose. Rather than stay hidden in the seclusion of the Judean Mountains or the obscurity of the Jordan River Valley, Jesus did what great leaders do: displayed courage in the face of adversity. Courage is "the quality of mind or spirit that enables a person to face difficulty, danger, or pain without fear." Jesus led the way toward the worst possible death with a scheming group of religious leaders lying in wait. Going to Jerusalem was a trap and the disciples knew it, which is why they were astonished and afraid while their Rabbi was full of resolve.

Sensing the apprehension among the followers, Jesus

pulled the 12 aside, and for the third and final time, laid out the plan. In leadership speak we call it "vision casting" and as always, Jesus' plans are rooted in the redemptive purpose of God. I can envision Jesus standing in the Jordan River Valley near Jericho looking westward at the massive mountains ahead on the road to Jerusalem. Roughly 20 miles away is the destination, and in that 20-mile stretch, the elevation rises from below sea level to roughly 3,000 feet. It is steep and will take its toll physically on Jesus' climbing companions. Add the mental and emotional stress of what lay ahead, and one is left with no doubt the journey will be trying.

Amid this backdrop, Jesus the leader makes the plan crystal clear. "We are going up to Jerusalem where I will be tried, tortured, and killed; but I will rise again." Though not recorded in this account, I can hear Jesus ask His followers as He points toward the mountains, "are you in?"

Following Jesus is not always easy, and sometimes the journey can take what looks like a turn for the worse. We have no clue why Jesus leads a certain way, no matter how clearly the vision is laid out. Like the disciples, we may find ourselves astonished and afraid of what may come, and we can stop, or quietly retreat to a place of comfort and security. But then, as we watch our Lord disappear over the mountainous terrain, we will find ourselves alone, and though we might miss out on a death, we will also miss out on a resurrection.

So often in my own life I have taken the road of safety and security rather than courageously following the more difficult plans and purposes of Christ. I may never know on this side of eternity what I missed out on. In the face of adversity, we really have three choices: stay put, retreat, or go up. What will it be?

Father, I have seen throughout this journey to the cross the challenges of discipleship. Now, as your Son calls me to climb with Him to Jerusalem, I find myself at a crossroads. I am prone to being fearful of the future and as a result, I often seek what is safe and comfortable. I also do not want to miss out on something great you have for my life because I refused to climb with Him. You always give the grace I need in the season I need it, and I need it now to go up to Jerusalem. In Christ's name, amen.

FIFTH SUNDAY OF LENT

"THE BAPTISM"

Reading: Mark 10:35-45

...Jesus said to them, "you will drink the cup I drink, and you will be baptized with the baptism I am baptized with."

MARK 10:39 (CSB)

I HAVE BEEN BAPTIZED three times in my life. The first time, I was 10 years old. Dad baptized me in the tank of our little church and all I knew at that point was baptism was what one did after saying the sinner's prayer. On a side note, I said that prayer nearly every week during my formative years just to make sure I was saved, and no sin was secretly lurking in the recesses of my young heart. The second baptism was in the southern section of the Jordan River near the Dead Sea. To make a long story short, a Pakistani pastor who went by the name "Lazarus" asked to be baptized as I was performing the sacrament for congregants from my church. After I baptized Lazarus, he asked to baptize me, and I agreed. Little did I know going into the water, I would literally be body-slammed face forward into the muddy Jordan. The video still lives somewhere on Instagram and Facebook.

The third baptism was at the northern Jordan site near Tiberias, and it was by far the most meaningful of the three. I was about four years removed from my dark night of the soul and had come to a full understanding of what it means to go through the waters of baptism and pass from death unto life, washing away the past, burying the old, and being resurrected into the new. It was an incredible moment I will never forget.

As the brothers Zebedee came to Jesus seeking power, prestige, and recognition, Jesus poignantly asked if they could drink the cup of His suffering and withstand the waters of His own baptism. Their reply was "yes," but much like my 10-year-old self, I wonder if they really understood what they said "yes" to. Baptism is indeed a passage from the old to the new, but it is also a type of the exodus from Egypt where we are freed from bondage and taken immediately into the wilderness where God forms and shapes our life and character to reflect His glory and prepare us for our calling.

Christ, after His own baptism, was driven by the Spirit into the wilderness to engage His full humanity with the temptations of the enemy and once He overcame, He went by the same Spirit to Nazareth to declare He was the Anointed One destined to bring God's Kingdom to Earth. James and John, two young fishermen from Galilee, were about to experience the full weight of Christ's baptism. In Jerusalem, they endured Christ's death following Him from Pilate's judgement hall to Golgotha's hill. John the Beloved stayed with Jesus until He breathed His last and outran Peter to the tomb on resurrection morning to experience the passage from death to life.

Then, the mission became theirs and through great wilderness testing, they went forth in the Spirit's power to change the world, not as prestigious rulers throwing their weight around, but as humble servants seeking to raise others up into a relationship with God. So, the next time we experience baptism, let us prepare for a wilderness that will take us from death to life, equipping us to minister to our world as servants of Christ. Only then can we truly say we are baptized with His baptism.

Father, I understand there cannot be a resurrection without a death. I admit today that difficulty is not my first choice, but I know it is through adversity you work your deepest work in my life. Today, I seek a fresh baptism, one that allows for renewal and being formed into the image of Christ. This formation will help me grow in you and prepare me for what you have called me to in this world. Do your work in me and through me. In Christ's name, amen.

TWENTY-NINTH DAY OF LENT
MONDAY
"THE MAN CALLED BARTIMAEUS"

Reading: Mark 10:46-52

Jesus sad to him, "Go, your faith has saved you." Immediately
he could see and began to follow Jesus on the road.

MARK 10:52 (CSB)

ALL THREE OF MY SONS were football players. Starting
in elementary school, they played into junior high and all the
way through high school. For the better part of 12 years, our
fall Fridays and Saturdays were dominated by gridiron action, and we loved every minute of it. My football career, on
the other hand, lasted three plays. I was a baseball guy, and
a pretty good one, but in 7th grade I decided to try football. I
started late in the preseason but landed a spot on a Pop Warner
feeder team for my local high school called the Sharks. They
stuck me at defensive tackle, and after weeks of practice, the
first game finally rolled around. For three-and-a-half quarters,
I stood on the sideline with helmet on, mouthpiece in, and the
hot September Arizona sun baking me inside the padded oven
I was wearing.

Finally, my name was called. I ran onto the field, assumed

the position and on the third play, I busted through the line in pursuit of the quarterback. Rolling to his left, the quarterback was dead to rights, and I had my sights set on a sack, but I took a bad angle and barely grazed him. The linebacker cleaned up my mess and we forced the punt. Three and out was the opposing team. Three and out was my football career as I decided to stick with baseball. I must admit, though, moving off the sideline and into the action for those three plays was exhilarating, and there is a part of me that regrets not going further.

For the Jericho resident called Bartimaeus, the sideline was his lot in life. As a blind beggar, he was outcast, ignored, and marginalized by the masses. On the busy road from Jericho to Jerusalem, hundreds of people each day passed by giving no thought to Bartimaeus the blind, lost, outcast, and hopeless as he begged for whatever he could get to sustain his meager existence.

When Bartimaeus heard Jesus was passing by on the way to Jerusalem, he knew this was his chance, his moment to encounter life-change, and that is exactly what happened. "Jesus, have mercy!" was the sincere cry which stopped Jesus in His tracks. From that moment on, Bartimaeus could no longer be called "Blind Bartimaeus," for he could now see, having been healed by Jesus. In this life-altering moment, Bartimaeus had a choice: stay on the sidelines or get in on the action. He chose the latter. He already acknowledged Jesus as Lord and Master by calling Him, "Rabboni," but as all disciples of Jesus realize, acknowledging Him is one thing. Following Him is another.

Bartimaeus had no idea of the journey Jesus and the disciples were on and what the road ahead would bring. He knew nothing of the religious leaders' plot or the pain and suffering which lay ahead, but he had been on the sideline for too long. He could have taken his new-found healing and gone another way, but he went the Jesus way "and began to follow Jesus on the road."

We know nothing else of Bartimaeus, but we learn from his example to never be content with our paralyzing circumstances. Jesus is passing our way, calling us from the sidelines into an action-filled new life. Taking the first step of faith with a heart-felt cry for mercy opens the door for salvation, but then it is up to us. Will we follow? Will we stay with our Rabboni, who holds all things in His hands? Sidelines or action? It's our call.

Father, I am grateful you heard my cry for mercy and stopped for me. I am grateful for allowing me to see when I was blind and grateful for the call to follow. May I never be content to take the wonderful gift of salvation you freely gave and go my own way. I need to go your way and follow you all the days of my life. Like Bartimaeus, I don't know what the road ahead will bring, but I trust you to lead, knowing the action of following is better than the inaction of the sidelines. In Christ's name, amen.

THIRTIETH DAY OF LENT
TUESDAY
"THE EVIDENCE"

Reading: Luke 19:1-10

When Jesus came to the place, he looked up and said to him, "Zacchaeus, hurry and come down because today it is necessary for me to stay at your house."

LUKE 19:5 (CSB)

IN THE MIDDLE of modern-day Jericho is a large sycamore fig tree dubbed, "The Zacchaeus Tree." Though the tree is old and well-grown, it is highly unlikely it was the actual tree the short chief tax collector climbed in his quest to see Jesus. It does, however, make for a great tourist stop and photo opportunity while passing through. Sycamore figs are massive trees, growing as high as 60 feet tall with strong branches spreading out wide, making an easy climb for one who wished to elevate above the crowd.

Zacchaeus' climb was a personal quest to see Jesus and his story reminds us just as our LORD looks upon the oppressed and lowly to raise them up, He also looks up at the mighty and proud. He invites them to come down from their personal, lofty perch to embrace the salvation which has come to the world through Jesus and offered to all. Throughout the gospels we never see Jesus in a hurry. Someone once wrote, "Jesus changed the world at 3 miles per hour," but in this case, Jesus was in fifth gear. "Don't waste any time, Zacchaeus, I am coming to your house. I'm inviting myself. Let's go!"

Though Luke does not elaborate on how it happened, we do know what happened. Something shifted in the heart of this despised man who was part of the wealthy elite of his day. The tax business in the first century was lucrative. Most at the top of the business pyramid were multi-level tax farmers with people working underneath, minions who extorted the poor for their bosses with hope of a better cut for themselves. Tax collectors could basically charge the citizens whatever they wanted if Rome got their portion. These men were hated by the masses and not even worthy to be named in the same category as sinners. That Jesus invited Himself into such a man's home defied all societal and religious norms, but Jesus came to save the lost, which means all the lost, the down and out as well as the up and out.

My contention is the moment Jesus called Zacchaeus by name, recognizing him as a person created in God's image, the diminutive tax collector was reminded of the imprint of God upon his life and the shift took place in his heart. Zacchaeus' name means "pure and innocent" and when Jesus spoke the name, it was a reminder the image of God upon his life, though tarnished, was not erased. We know this because of the evidence.

From this moment forward, Zacchaeus' life was no longer marked by the self-centered way of the tax collectors, but by being centered on others. He liquidated assets to give away to those in need and made restitution to those he extorted at an interest rate of 400%. That is evidence of a changed life, a life which no longer elevates self, but others. Once God calls our name, may we respond with haste and come down from our self-supporting branches. Doing so positions us to be loved and supported by the One who will soon hang from a branch so we can be reconciled to God and live a life centered around others.

Father, today we look at the many ways we create our own support branches without staying connected to you. We are prone to leaning on ourselves, but we recognize this kind of self-sufficiency is not sustainable. We must always allow our branches to be grafted into you. When we abide in you, we bear fruit and your wonderful image stamped upon our lives will then reflect your glory in greater measure. Like Zacchaeus, may the change within result in a greater heart toward others. We seek this today in Christ's name, amen.

THIRTY-FIRST DAY OF LENT
WEDNESDAY
"THE ANOINTING AT BETHANY"

Reading: John 12:1-8

Jesus answered, 'Leave her alone; she has kept it for the day of my burial.'

JOHN 12:7 (CSB)

IN THE FALL OF 1934, a fiery evangelist by the name of Mordecai Ham held a series of revival meetings in a make-shift tabernacle in Charlotte, North Carolina. Twice a day, six days per week for 11 weeks, Ham thundered the gospel message as thousands flocked to the sawdust-floored building. On November 7 that same year, a young, lanky boy just shy of his 16th birthday responded to Ham's message from Romans.

But God commendeth his love toward us, in that, while we were yet sinners, Christ died for us.
(Romans 5:8 KJV)

That night, the young teenager said "yes" to Jesus and began a new life in Christ.

You may have never heard of Mordecai Ham, but odds

are, you have heard of the young man who committed his life to Christ that night. His name was Billy Graham. Graham died in 2018 but left a legacy as one of the greatest evangelists in church history, and one of the most influential figures of the 20th century. Millions across the world said "yes" to Jesus after either attending or watching one of his evangelistic crusades on television, and Graham became a spiritual friend and advisor to several U.S. presidents. There is little doubt, if not for Mordecai Ham's obedience to the call of God and act of faithfulness to preach the gospel, Graham's story may have been different. Acts of faith and devotion to God indeed have ripple effects which echo through eternity.

Mary's act of devotion and love at a Sabbath dinner in Bethany on the eve of the Passion Week is like that. The lavish outpouring of a perfume worth a year's wages; the sincere overflow of gratitude toward her LORD; the culturally unacceptable practice of letting down her hair to wipe the extended feet of Jesus as He reclined at the table, are all examples inviting us to give our best, pour out our love, and shamelessly worship our King. The ripple effects of this moment cannot be understated.

The narrative gives no indication Mary knew the fate awaiting Jesus in the coming week but like Caiaphas and his unknowing prophecy of the death of Christ being for all people, Mary's act of devotion is written into the gospel story to unveil how God works through us to impact eternity. Mark's account of this story reveals a powerful proclamation by Jesus of Mary's act of faith and devotion.

> Truly I tell you, wherever the gospel is proclaimed in the whole world, what she has done will also be told in memory of her.
> (Mark 14:9 CSB)

When we give acts of faith and devotion to God, we may never know the eternal ripple effects these acts may have, but our story will be recorded in the chronicles of eternity. Like Mary the sister of Lazarus and Mordecai Ham the evangelist, we have one job – to be obedient and pour out our lives freely and selflessly to God and humanity. In doing so, we not only touch the heart of our Savior, but we could also be touching the heart of the next Billy Graham.

Father, forgive me for the times I have been careless about how I live my life. May I become more aware of my daily actions and ponder the ripple effects. Actions that fail to glorify you can negatively affect others, but the reverse is true. Actions which glorify you have the potential to change eternity. Give me the grace to slow down and think before I act – how will this glorify you and impact eternity? I won't always get it right, but today I commit to pausing and reflecting. May my life truly glorify you in both word and deed. In Christ's name, amen.

THIRTY-SECOND DAY OF LENT
THURSDAY
"THE PLOT TO KILL LAZARUS"

Reading: John 12:9-11

...because he was the reason many of the Jews were deserting them and believing in Jesus.

JOHN 12:11 (CSB)

ONE OF THE GREATEST moments in U.S. sports history took place February 22, 1980, when a group of young college hockey players upset the Soviet Union, the greatest team of the era, in the Olympic medal round. The game hails its legacy as "The Miracle on Ice," and rightly so. If those two teams played 100 times, the Soviets would have probably won 99, but on that cold, wintry night in Lake Placid, New York, a miracle indeed took place. Recent documentaries told from the Russians' point of view paint a different picture. The former Soviet players contend they lost to the Americans because of overconfidence and bad coaching, thereby making the miracle to be less than it was.

Even when God does something miraculous in our lives, not everyone will stick around for the confetti. Hardened or jealous hearts will downplay our miracle with condescending tones and obvious indifference. Don't get me wrong, many will rejoice and be changed by our story, but others will care less.

Lazarus was a walking miracle. He died and for four days, lay in the grave until his friend, Jesus, showed up and called him forth, raising him from death unto life. It was an undeniable miracle that caused many to start following Jesus. Crowds flocked to the tiny village of Bethany to see Jesus and the one who had been dead, now alive. The chief priests, however, were less than enthused as their entire religious, political, and social system now stood on the brink of collapse. They were being deserted for a Galilean rabbi. Blinded by their own pride and insecurities, these religious leaders could not embrace a true, living testimony of the grace and goodness of God. Having already decided to kill Jesus, their plot now expanded to take out Lazarus. "If we can't kill Jesus, at the very least we can kill one of the reasons people are going after Him."

Our world is so blinded from the truth, it cannot see who Jesus really is. Some wish Jesus and Christianity would just go away and fade into oblivion to become a relic of history. But, if they cannot get rid of Jesus, they will go after us for we are the living representatives of Christ on Earth. We have passed from death unto life and bear the tangible, miraculous proof something lost can indeed be found. We were dead in trespasses and sins, but God who is rich in mercy raised us up. Bound by sin, our chains were broken, and Christ set us free. We were once children of disobedience, but now we live, walk, and model a better way. We cannot be discouraged when others will not participate in our miracle.

I am not convinced the religious leaders hated Lazarus. They hated what he represented. Jesus declared we would be hated because of Him (Matt. 10:22), but that does not negate what He has done in our lives. The Resurrection and the Life miraculously raised us, and the victory is ours. No matter how the naysayers spin it, we are living, breathing miracles because of Him. Let them try and take us out. Go for it. We have already won.

Father, today I rejoice for the miracle of salvation. You have brought me from death unto life, and whether people see it or not, I recognize it and stand grateful for all you have done. I choose today to own my story and declare it boldly knowing there is no power in heaven, hell, or on Earth which can negate the work you have done in my life. You rewrote my story, and as long as I have breath, I will testify to your goodness.

In Christ's name, amen.

THIRTY-THIRD DAY OF LENT
FRIDAY
"THE JOY SET BEFORE HIM"

Reading: Hebrews 12:1-2

...fixing our eyes on Jesus, the author and perfecter of faith, who for the joy set before Him endured the cross, despising the shame, and has sat down at the right hand of the throne of God.

HEBREWS 12:2 (NAS)

THE STAGE IS SET for Passion Week, the hinge-point of history. The final journey of Christ to Jerusalem which began at Caesarea Philippi nears its conclusion. With the finish line in sight and knowing full-well what lies ahead, Jesus is prepared. Three times on this journey to the cross, Jesus drew His disciples aside to let them know what is coming – arrest, trial, suffering, and death on a cross. The 12 lacked a full understanding of what Jesus spoke about, but they knew their LORD had set His face toward Jerusalem. Though many followed along the way, the opposition from the religious leaders was strong, and Jesus remained undeterred in His purpose and mission.

The writer of Hebrews declares there was joy set before our LORD which enabled Him to endure the cross and despise the shame of hanging naked on a tree, dying an undeserved criminal's death. How could Jesus find joy amid the expectation of pain and humiliation? Being fully human, waves of emotion surely flooded His soul, for no human being could possibly rejoice at the prospect of a torturous flogging and humiliating death.

The reality is, Jesus saw joy as the *end* of the journey. In the Hebrew worldview, joy, also meaning grace, blessing, and favor, is meant to be shared with others and not kept to oneself. The joy set before Christ at the end of the journey was not a personal quest for inner happiness, but a joy He would share with all creation benefitting from His selfless act of suffering and death. There is an old gospel song titled "When He was on the Cross, I was on His Mind," which although encouraging, is a bit narcissistic. The joy set before Christ was the salvation of the cosmos, which opened the door for all humanity to be reconciled to God and all the wrongs caused by sin in the created order to be made right. What God accomplished in Christ, despite the horrors of suffering, changed the trajectory of a created ordered spiraling toward non-existence and set the course back toward God. It was the joy set before Him, to be shared with all, which gave Christ the strength to endure.

As we take up our cross and live under the banner of a cruciform life, God is accomplishing the restoration of all things through us, His redeemed people. The race we run is not a sprint. It is a marathon for which we lay aside weight and besetting sin to run with the same endurance Christ possessed as He neared the finish line. There may be no inherent joy in the challenges we face on our personal journey, but if we keep our eyes fixed on Jesus and follow His example, we will see the joy that all things are working for good.

Somehow, our journey fits into the redemptive purposes of God. Somehow, every roadblock we face is an opportunity for us to lean unto Jesus as He perfects our faith for the benefit of a world that needs to see the finished work of Christ active in His plan for creation. Maybe with this approach, we can move away from a self-centered faith to a faith where we all share the joy of knowing in the end, all will be made right.

Father, today as I reflect on the joy set before Christ on the eve of the passion week, prepare my heart to finish the journey to the cross. In this upcoming Holy Week, turn my eyes to Christ and Christ alone. May all my senses be finely tuned to experience the full weight of this week with Him. May I experience the true glory of the cross and all it represents for the created order, and as a result, may I come to a fuller understanding of what it means to live under the banner of a cruciform life. In Christ's name, amen.

THIRTY-FOURTH DAY OF LENT
SATURDAY
"THE PREPARATION"

TODAY WE STAND on the eve of Passion Week. I invite you to use today as a day of reflection and preparation and use the three historical prayers which follow to center the attention of your mind and the affection of your heart upon our LORD and Savior. As we prayed together yesterday, this coming week, may we come to a fuller understanding of what it means to live under the banner of a cruciform life.

Breathe in me, O Holy Spirit, that my thoughts may all be holy. Act in me, O Holy Spirit, that my work, too, may be holy. Draw my heart, O Holy Spirit, that I may love only what is holy. Strengthen me, O Holy Spirit, that I may defend all that is holy. Guard me, O Holy Spirit, that I myself may always be holy. Amen. (Augustine of Hippo)

O merciful Father do not consider what we have done against you; but what our blessed Savior has done for us. Don't consider what we have made of ourselves, but what He is making of us for you our God. O that Christ may be "wisdom and righteousness, sanctification and redemption" to every one of our souls. May His precious blood cleanse us from all our sins, and your Holy Spirit renew and sanctify our souls. May He crucify our flesh with its passion and lusts and cleanse all our brothers and sisters in Christ across the earth. Amen. (John Wesley)

I Cannot Do This Alone O God. Early in the morning I cry to you. Help me to pray and to concentrate my thoughts on you; I cannot do this alone. In me there is darkness, but with you there is light; I am lonely, but you do not leave me; I am feeble in heart, but with you there is help; I am restless, but with you there is peace. In me there is bitterness, but with you there is patience; I do not understand your ways, but you know the way for me.... Restore me to liberty, and enable me to live now that I may answer before you and before men. Lord whatever this day may bring, Your name be praised. Amen. (Deitrich Bonhoeffer)

PASSION WEEK
PALM SUNDAY
"THE TRIUMPHAL ENTRY"

Reading: Matthew 21:1-11

Tell daughter Zion, 'see, your King is coming to you, gentle, and mounted on a donkey, and on a colt, the foal of a donkey.'

MATTHEW 21:5 (CSB)

TODAY WE CELEBRATE what is traditionally called "Palm Sunday," and it marks the beginning of the final days of Christ on the Earth. Five hundred years before the birth of Jesus, the prophet Zechariah saw this day coming and Matthew records the words of his prophetic declaration. "Behold, your King is coming to you." (Zech. 9:9) As Jesus descended the steep slope on the western edge of the Mount of Olives riding the foal of a donkey, crowds gathered. Flanking the pathway, His followers spread their clothes along the road and in the words of John's gospel…

…they took palm branches and went out to meet him. They kept shouting: 'Hosanna! Blessed is he who comes in the name of the Lord.' (John 12:13 CSB)

The shouts of 'Hosanna' came from Psalm 118, a song traditionally sung at Passover, reveling in the day God set aside to exalt the rejected cornerstone. As the celebration continued toward the city of Jerusalem, the was no doubt what was happening. Jesus' followers saw this as a coronation day for their King, and I find it interesting that Jesus did not fight it. In fact, when the religious leaders told our LORD to silence His followers, the King's reply was:

> ...if they were to keep silent, the stones would cry out.
> (Luke 19:40 CSB)

This was a statement moment for the King, but not in the way His followers assumed. For the followers of Jesus, it was a revolutionary, military triumph. "At last…our King is here to defeat Rome, take the throne away from the corrupt Herodians, return it to the line of David, and restore the Kingdom of Israel to its former glory." Jesus, however, is a different kind of King. He doesn't ride a Roman stallion war horse or command the armies of heaven to lay waste His enemies. He doesn't revel in the spotlight and demand all bow before His earthly splendor and might. Oh, make no mistake, every knee will bow to the King of Kings, but today is not that day. Today, He rides a donkey and prepares to lay waste to different enemies – sin and death.

Palm Sunday and the rest of the days of Holy Week reinforce this truth: even when we don't come to Him, our King comes to us. "Tell daughter Zion, your King is coming to you!" This is the heart of the gospel, the life of God coming to us. Our unassuming King comes to us because He loves us, which is the reason He came. God so loved the world, that He gave His Son (John 3:16). He demonstrated this love in that while we were still sinners, Christ died for us (Romans 5:8). Because of this great love, we were made alive, even though we were dead in trespasses and sin (Ephesians 2:1-10).

As Jesus rode onward to Jerusalem, He knew what was ahead. The King was coming, not to overthrow an Empire, but to make those bound by the burden of death alive unto God. Be encouraged today. Whatever you may be facing in life, whatever struggles you have, whatever burdens you carry, your King is coming to you. He is pursuing you because He loves you. That is a different kind of King.

Almighty and eternal God, in your tender love towards humanity you sent your Son, our Savior Jesus Christ to take on himself our flesh and to suffer death on the cross. Grant that we may follow the example of his patience and humility, and also be made partakers of his resurrection; through your Son, Jesus Christ our LORD, who lives and reigns with you and the Holy Spirit, one God, now and forever. In Christ's name, amen.

(Adapted from Book of Common Prayer/Common Worship, after Gelasian, historic collect for Palm Sunday)

PASSION WEEK
THIRTY-FIFTH DAY OF LENT
MONDAY
"THE OVERTURNING"

Reading: Mark 11:15-19

...He overturned the tables of the moneychangers, and the chairs of those selling doves.

MARK 11:15 (CSB)

CHURCH IS A MACHINE. At least, it can be. Having pastored small, mid-sized, and large congregations, I am fully aware of day-to-day operations and what it takes to keep a church running. Buildings, budgets, and backsides can consume church leaders during the week and there are constant pressures with running the machine that, if we are not cautious, can cause us to lose sight of the mission. We can become so possessed with the what, where, when, and how, we forget the why.

Even Sunday can become a machine. Several years ago, I arrived at church early on Sunday morning (which is normal for me) and in those days, I usually wore gym shorts or joggers and a t-shirt, carrying my change of clothes for service separately. On this day, it was about an hour before church and I sat comfortably at my desk, feet up, just chilling before the action began. A staff member arrived dressed full-on for church and looked at me in shock because I wasn't ready. My response was arrogant and flippant – "Sunday comes every seven days."

Later that day, reflecting on my snarky comment, I realized I had fallen into the trap of keeping the machine going while losing sight of the why. For me, it was just another Sunday, just another day to preach, count the people, count the offering, and go home. I had to repent and ask Jesus to overturn this attitude in my heart and reorient me to the why. This is what happened on the second day of Passion Week when Jesus entered the temple.

Herod's Temple was a massive, opulent structure capable of handling thousands of people in its outer courts where the machine of ministry set up shop. There were sacrifices to be made and major feasts such as Passover meant major opportunity. It was basic supply and demand. Demand for sacrifices go up, prices go up and the ones most affected are the poor and marginalized. The Sanhedrin were happy during these seasons as their annual Temple budget was met and the leaders rested calmly knowing the machine they created would keep running.

Once Jesus, this different kind of King, entered the courtyard, He knew things had to change. Overturning the tables and chairs of the moneychangers sent a message that the old order of things was being flipped upside down. Selfishness and greed fueling the machine had squeezed the life from the mission of God. The outer courts of the Temple were designed to be a place where every tribe, tongue, and nation had the opportunity to connect with God and have their lives transformed. Calling the machine operators "robbers" implied something far greater than stealing money and extorting the poor. Robbers were revolutionaries who tried to overturn God's mission for the nations and Jesus would have none of it.

The message from Jesus is clear that mission trumps all and God's redemptive purpose is far greater than any machine can stop. Maybe we need Jesus to come in and flip over tables in our own heart which hinder His mission from taking priority. Whatever impedes us from connecting with God, maybe it's time for a revolutionary King to overturn it.

O Father, most merciful, in the beginning you created us, and by the passion of your only Son, you created us anew. Work in us now, both to will and to do what pleases you. Since we are weak and can do no good thing by ourselves, grant us your grace and heavenly blessing, that in whatever work we engage we may do all to your honor and glory. Keep us from sin and empower us daily to do good works, that as long as we live in the body we may always perform service to you. Since you have given us pardon of all our sins, after our departure receive us to eternal life; through him who lives and reigns with you and the Holy Spirit, for ever and ever. In Christ's name, amen.

(St. Anselm, 11th-century prayer for Holy Week)

PASSION WEEK
THIRTY-SIXTH DAY OF LENT
TUESDAY
"THE EXAMPLE"

Reading: John 13:1-17

For I have given you an example, that you also should do just
as I have done for you.

JOHN 13:15 (CSB)

I AM PRONE TO MISS THE OBVIOUS. More than once
in my married life, Gwen has sent me on a fishing expedition
into the abyss of her purse or the cavernous recesses of the
medicine cabinet to locate a simple item — hand sanitizer,
band-aids, vitamins, keys, tissue, or anything from an endless
list of everyday things. Inevitably it turns into a lengthy ordeal
which forces me to take everything out of the purse or cabinet,
and the results are always the same: "Can't find it, babe!" My
gracious wife will come to my aid, and with a single opening
of the purse or cabinet, pull the item. "Here it is! Right in front
of your face in plain sight." I missed the obvious.

Seeing does not always guarantee recognition. Often in
life, we need others to point out the obvious and the response
should be as clear as "Here it is!" For three-and-a-half years,

Jesus mentored His closest followers to follow His ways. He taught them with practical stories relating to everyday life, challenged them to take ownership of their own lives, and reminded them of the real cost of discipleship. He modeled love for God and neighbor, paring the Torah down to these two things, but they still didn't get it. They missed the obvious, much to Jesus' frustration. Now, 24 hours prior to being placed in a borrowed tomb, Jesus provides His inner circle with a "here it is" moment.

Stripped of His outer garment and girded with a towel, Christ performs the most menial task of servanthood and washes the feet of the 12, including Judas who would soon sell Him out to the religious leaders. John does not record every detail of this life-changing act, but Peter's response was indicative of what the others in the room were certainly processing. "You're not doing this, LORD," to which Jesus replied,

> ...if I don't wash you, you can't be part of what I'm doing.
> (John 13:8b MSG)

Jesus was saying to Peter and the rest of the 12, "If you want to be relationally connected to me and what I am doing in the world, I have to do this."

Staying connected to Jesus means staying connected not only to His ways, but also to His purpose. With full humility on display, our LORD puts forth exactly what this entails. Followers of Jesus serve. Period. They take the lower position, give up the best seats at the table, rid themselves of pride and ego to serve. This is the example He left for us and it's in plain sight, right here in front of our faces. "Now," Jesus said, "do just as I have done for you."

The greatest commandment is love, and love serves. It serves God with a committed heart, a renewed mind, and a fortified strength that comes only from Him. Love serves our neighbors with actions that will cause them to pause and see in plain sight a true example of Christ. Let's not make the world go on a scavenger hunt to see Jesus. Let's wrap up in a towel, grab a basin of water, and serve.

O Lord Jesus Christ, Son of man, you did not come to be served, but to serve. Give us grace to lay aside all our vanity, clothe us with your power, and crown us with your humility, that finally, in the glory of serving, we may stand beside your throne, where with the Father and the Holy Spirit you reign, one God, now and forever. In Christ's name, amen.

(John Wallace Suter, 1919)

PASSION WEEK
THIRTY-SEVENTH DAY OF LENT
HOLY WEDNESDAY
"THE LAST SUPPER"

Reading: Luke 22:14-23

And he took bread, gave thanks, broke it, gave it to them
and said, "This is my body, which is given for you. Do
this in remembrance of me."
LUKE 22:19 (CSB)

THE PRE-PASSOVER MEAL progresses. Jesus, the example, continues to impart life-changing truth to the 11 men who will change the world. John's Gospel records more in-depth conversations about the Holy Spirit and His role to be played in the life of Christ's followers, but ironically, does not discuss the Eucharist which is left to the other three gospel writers.

Discussion of the Eucharist, what it means, and how it functions in the life and practice of the Church has spawned debates, theological writings, and branches of the Reformation. Some expressions of Christianity believe the bread and cup become the body and blood of Christ and this is practiced each time the church gathers. Other expressions see the meal as a symbol, a memorial of sorts, which affords believers the opportunity to reflect upon what Christ did on the cross. Regardless of its lived expression, "Do this in remembrance of me" was the command of Christ concerning this Holy moment. We must, however, look at the context of the evening in which Jesus established this practice for His followers.

For Israel, the Passover feast was a celebration of deliverance and hope. At the beginning of the meal, the children of the house asked the question of the elders, "why is this night different from all the others?" The answer evoked a solemn time in which God's people recalled their deliverance from Egypt and how Yahweh intervened on their behalf, showing His might, and leaving no doubt who was the Supreme God. They recalled other times in their history when God intervened to bring deliverance and looked forward to the day when the final deliverance will take place, and all will be made right. Passover night was about remembering the past while instilling hope for the future amid the present reality. Church historian, Justo Gonzales, frames it brilliantly.

"The Passover is a celebration of the certain hope that the God who brought the people out of Egypt will again lead the people into renewal, life, and freedom." (Commentary on Luke)

Jesus used this powerful celebration of deliverance and hope to bring His followers to a prepared table that brings the past deliverance and future hope to a present reality. The disciples became active participants in what God had done, is doing, and will do. Christ's work on the cross will guarantee the availability of salvation and deliverance for all, not only from sin, but also from the oppressive systems of man which draw people into bondage. By eating the broken bread and drinking the fruit of the vine, we share in Christ's suffering and redemptive work and whether we realize it or not, we say "yes" to our lives being poured out for others who need deliverance and hope.

When we "do this" in remembrance of Him, we enter His redemptive mission and become the agents of His work on Earth. We bring our lives as wheat from the field. He breaks us and grinds us into bread which becomes nourishment for the souls of humanity, just as He was crushed to become the Bread of Life. We bring our lives as grapes from the vine through our own trials to be crushed into wine that is then poured out to a world that needs the hope only Christ can bring.

"Doing this" involves so much more than elements and entering endless debates on how Christ is present. When I receive the Eucharist, I willingly receive what Christ did, but I also enter what Christ is doing so I can bring the hope of what He will do in the Earth. We must rid ourselves of symbolic juice and cracker thinking and remember each time we gather to share this Holy meal, we are "doing this." Theologian Karl Rahner wonderfully captures this missional aspect of the Eucharist.

"From the last supper there stretches the unbroken chain of all those whom Jesus has sent out on His mission with His word. Link after link falls into place in this succession of living

bread and the earthly wine, the chain of human words
and human signs."
(Biblical Homilies, Foristal and Strachan, 1966, 52)

This night is different than other nights because in Christ, God brings a past deliverance and future hope into a present reality. Christ will do what no other can do, and once done, we are invited then to do this in remembrance of Him.

I am no longer my own, but yours. Put me to what you will, place me with whom you will. Put me to doing, put me to suffering. Let me be put to work for you or set aside for you, praised for you, or criticized for you. Let me be full, let me be empty. Let me have all things, let me have nothing. I freely and fully surrender all things to your glory and service. And now, O wonderful and holy God, Creator, Redeemer, and Sustainer, You are mine, and I am yours. So be it. And the covenant which I have made on earth, let it also be made in heaven. In Christ's name, amen. (Wesley's Covenant Prayer)

PASSION WEEK
THIRTY-EIGHTH DAY OF LENT
MAUNDY THURSDAY
"THE GARDEN OF GETHSEMANE"

Reading: Matthew 26:36-56

...then all the disciples deserted him and ran away.

MATTHEW 26:56 (CSB)

JUST EAST OF THE KIDRON VALLEY across from the old city of Jerusalem stands the Church of All Nations, also known as the Basilica of Agony. This beautiful, solemn edifice was built by the Franciscans in 1924 over the traditional site where Christ prayed in Gethsemane. Adjacent to the church is a small grove of ancient olive trees, most likely descendants of the first-century forebears, along with a secluded place to pray and reflect on the passion of Christ which began in earnest nearby.

When my wife and I visited Israel for the third time in 2023, we had a powerful prayer time in Gethsemane, following Christ's example, and renewing our personal commitment to do the Father's will above all else in our lives. Making our way from there into the stunning church, we allowed the interior art of the Basilica to tell the story of what happened that fateful night in Gethsemane. There is the flat stone in the Basilica's center where the agony of Christ was so great, His sweat became drops of blood while His friends slept. Beautiful paintings retell the kiss of betrayal by Judas and the subsequent arrest by the Temple Guard as Peter, James, and John watched from a distance "that all the writings of the prophets would be fulfilled."

Coming out of the church, I looked atop the building and noticed two bronze deer flanking the cross on either side. Immediately, my mind went to Psalm 42:1.

As the deer pants for streams of water, so my soul pants for you, my God (NIV)

It was as if the two deer were drinking life-giving water from the cross of Christ. Adding to the wonder of this image, I noticed the mosaic on the façade of the church depicting Jesus' arms outstretched between God and man. On His left is a woman with a dying child in her arms and on His right stand the rich and powerful of the Earth. The message of this mosaic was clear. All, both poor and rich, cry out in their own agony to the Son who, through His own agony and suffering, builds a bridge between the human condition and Divine hope. Beneath this powerful image on the Basilica, in Latin, Hebrews 5:7 is inscribed.

He offered up prayers and petitions with fervent cries and tears
to the one who could save him from death, and he was heard
because of his reverent submission. (NIV)

The connection to Gethsemane on the night of Jesus' betrayal is not lost. Because of Christ's agony, intercession, and self-giving, loving sacrifice, we who are thirsty and long for God can cross the bridge His mercy built. Like the deer, we then stand at the foot of the cross and drink from the fountain flowing from Emmanuel's veins. The cup Christ drank that night in Gethsemane was a cup of intercession and it was all for us. No other could drink it. It was His alone to drink and it was the will of the Father so all who agonize and are thirsty can come. Because of His agony, He takes our agony and bring us to Himself so we can be reconciled to God.

Lord, when I face the crosses of my own life, give me Your divine courage and strength to say "Yes" to the will of the Father. Your love for me is abundant and is perfect in every way. Help me to know that love, to embrace it and to allow it into my life. In Christ's name, amen.
(Prayers for Holy Thursday)

PASSION WEEK
THIRTY-NINTH DAY OF LENT
GOOD FRIDAY
"THE DEATH"

Reading: John 19:1-37

When Jesus received the sour wine, he said, 'it is finished.' Then bowing his head, he gave up his spirit.

JOHN 19:30 (CSB)

ON GOOD FRIDAY we celebrate the cross of Jesus Christ as the epicenter of our faith. This is the gospel, the good news we proclaim: the Creator of the universe who spoke the worlds into existence took on human flesh in the Person of His Son, Jesus Christ. Though innocent of any wrongdoing, Jesus was tried, convicted, and sentenced to death by the most horrific, shameful means a person could die – crucifixion. To de-emphasize the cross of Christ in any way is nothing more than an outright betrayal of the One who suffered upon it and despised its shame.

To contemplate the cross of Jesus Christ is not only a way to remember what was done, but also a way to enter a sacred mystery which demonstrates the greatest attribute of God – love. Yes, the cross is the ultimate display of God's self-revelation. It is the place where Jesus made a public spectacle of Satan along with all principalities and powers. The cross is the death by which Christ conquers death and forgives sin as He becomes one with human suffering. Make no mistake as we contemplate all the cross is. It is the supreme demonstration of the love of God. Rightly said, because of Christ's death, the world now revolves around an axis of love.

When Jesus spoke His final words, "it is finished," He willingly gave up His spirit to the Father and God's redemptive plan from ages past became a present reality providing hope for the future under the banner of everlasting love. Some may ask, "if the cross was truly a finishing act, why is there still pain and suffering in the world? What does 'it is finished' really imply?" The word used for "finished" is *tetelestai* in the original language, meaning "accomplished" or "fulfilled."

First, the cross is the fulfillment of all that came before. The finished work did not commence on Good Friday, but as my Old Testament professor said my first day of Bible College, "it was conceived in the mind of God from the beginning of creation." The finished work proceeded from the fall in the Garden of Eden through the promises given to the patriarchs and confirmed by the prophets. It came to Earth in a Bethlehem cave and was announced at a Nazareth Synagogue where it was declared "this is the year of God's favor..." (Luke 4), meaning redemption for all had come.

Second, "it is finished" embodies a present reality whereby we enter all it provides with the opportunity to daily put to death our old self and practices, clothing ourselves with love, which binds everything in perfect unity (Colossians 3:5, 9-14). Good Friday is good because "it is finished" both completes and establishes.

As we look today upon the One who suffered, hangs on a cross, and is pierced for our transgressions, may we also contemplate what really happened. A work was finished, and the reality of the finished work is embodied through us as we press toward the day when all will be made right. It is only possible through the One who willingly gave all so we could receive all.

May your abundant blessing, Lord, come down upon your people who have devoutly recalled the death of your Son in the sure and certain hope of their resurrection: grant them pardon, bring them comfort, may their faith grow stronger, and their eternal salvation be assured; through Jesus Christ our Lord, amen.

(From the Scottish Presbyterian Good Friday Liturgy)

PASSION WEEK
FORTIETH DAY OF LENT
HOLY SATURDAY
"THE BURIAL"

Reading: John 19:38-42

For I passed on to you as most important...that Christ died for
our sins according to the scriptures, that he was buried...

1 CORINTHIANS 15:3-4a (CSB)

OUR JOURNEY TO THE CROSS has come to an end and
Jesus is dead. He died because of our sins. We put Him on
the cross, but He willingly gave up His spirit to the Father.
That Christ was on the cross for about six hours is miraculous
as many condemned criminals hung on their crosses for days
awaiting the Roman soldiers to mercifully break their legs and
hasten death. Jesus, however, was in complete control and
when the soldier came to accelerate His exit from this world,
Jesus was already dead, having breathed His last.

What Joseph of Arimathea and Nicodemus did in this moment was critical. They took the lifeless body of Jesus, prepared it for burial according to custom, wrapped it in a linen
cloth, placed it in a tomb and sealed it shut. One does not
do this to a person who lives, but only to one who has truly

died. Jesus is dead and, thus, begins Holy Saturday, the day between.

We know now what nobody knew then – a resurrection is coming, but Jesus did not feign death to stage a fake resurrection. He rose again because He died and was buried, yet nobody anticipated a resurrection would come. Nobody. From their perspective, when Jesus died, it was over, and His followers had nothing left to do except find a way to move on with life. The 11 disciples went into hiding for fear they would be next, hunted down by the Sanhedrin to suffer the same fate as their Rabbi. The rest of Christ's followers went home to their villages and cities to grieve the loss and figure out what was next.

For us, knowing what happens next, Saturday is the day between. It is the day between…

Despair and Hope

Tragedy and Triumph

Defeat and Victory

Sorrow and Jubilation

Saturday is the day between a death and a resurrection where we wait, process, grieve, pray, and hope. When life comes to a screeching halt and everything falls apart, it feels like a death, and it feels final. Experiencing great loss forces us to find a way through our pain. In these moments, we recall Christ willingly entered death to defeat death and His burial is a reminder that He stands in solidarity with us when we have packed up our hopes and dreams and tucked them neatly away to try and move on.

The good news is, we can move on because we know something now the ancients would soon discover. Christ died and He was buried, but because of this, tomorrow is a new day. As we wait in the darkness of Saturday, we grieve the loss, but we do not grieve as those who have no hope for unless there is a death and burial, there cannot be a resurrection. Don't fear Saturday in light of Friday. Embrace Saturday anticipating hope only Sunday can bring.

O God, Creator of heaven and earth: Grant that, as the crucified body of your dear Son was laid in the tomb and rested on this holy Sabbath, so we may await with him the coming of the third day, and rise with him to newness of life; who now lives and reigns with you and the Holy Spirit, one God, for ever and ever. In Christ's name, amen.

(From the Book of Common Prayer)

EASTER SUNDAY

Very early in the morning, on the first day of the week, they went to the tomb at sunrise. They were saying to one another, "Who will roll away the stone from the entrance to the tomb for us?" Looking up, they noticed that the stone — which was very large — had been rolled away.

MARK 16:2-4 (CSB)

OUR LENTEN JOURNEY is complete. The 50-day season of Pentecost has begun. The next volume in *The Journey Devotional Series, Journey to the Harvest*, begins with an Easter Sunday reflection and continues through to the Day of Pentecost when the Spirit of God is poured out upon His people, and we celebrate the harvest.

Father, I thank you for these past days of fasting, prayer, reflection, and deepening discipleship. I have sensed your presence every step of the way and stand grateful for your Son, Jesus Christ, and His finished work upon the cross. I commit my life this day forward to taking up my cross and following you whole-heartedly, to serve humanity with the great love you have shown toward me. By your Spirit, I can do all things through Christ who gives me the strength. In Christ's name, amen.

ACKNOWLEDGEMENTS

There are so many people in my life that made contributions to this work. This is by no means an exhaustive list, and the words that follow cannot fully express my gratitude to these incredible individuals, but they come from my heart.

To my wife and family for believing in me. Without them, this book would have never happened.

To my sister, Julie Miser, for her tireless work on the graphics and formatting. She is a true pro.

To my editor, Judy Hilovsky, for helping me understand how to use the word "that."

To everyone who walked with me all the way through my dark night of the soul. You know who you are, and I am grateful for your friendship.

To my dad, Gene, for always modeling the way of Christ.

Finally, to my mom, Patricia, who is watching from heaven. Your passion for scripture was imparted to me when I was a young boy. I miss you....

Made in the USA
Las Vegas, NV
21 February 2024

86016625R00090